To the women who want to know their men.

To the men who need to know their women.

REMEMBER:

> your *Choices*,
>
> the *Characteristics* you look for,
>
> any *Compromises* you are willing to make,
>
> helping to *Conform* his past behavior,
>
> and learning about your areas of *Compatibility*,

all lead up to a simple *Challenge* to teach your Mr. Right, using the concept of learned behavior and proven strategies, how to be and stay romantic, and enable you to measure his progress using the *Charts* I've outlined in this book.

Happy Reading!

Keith Hammond

Romance 101

Class Is In Session

Cover Layout and Interior Design: Keith Hammond
3D characters on cover from well-known software

uality Of Life oks

Romance101book.com

IMPRINT A Quality Of Life Book

Romance 101
Class Is In Session

© 2012 by
Keith Hammond
is published by
Lessons For Life Books, Inc.
7455 France Ave. S. #305
Edina, MN 55435

Inquiries should be addressed in writing to:
Lessons For Life Books
7455 France Avenue South #305
Edina, MN 55435
or by email to:
author@LessonsForLifeBooks.com

ISBN-13: 978-1-482570-63-2
Library of Congress Control Number:
Printed in the U.S.A.

Dedication

To my family

Annie, my wife,
the woman I've been with for 29 years.
Thank you for letting me be
romantic, passionate, chivalrous, spontaneous,
and incredibly mannish all these years.

Rochelle, my daughter
Kisha, my daughter
Now you know what to look for
in the men you marry.

To my son-in-law Carlos
Knowledge truly is power..

Acknowledgement

*There are many people who at some point and time of my life,
made a measurable impact, whether good or bad,
I am thankful for your input into me,
as it helped God prune, grow and mature me in more ways,
than you will ever know.*

God Bless You All.

TABLE OF CONTENTS

Romance 101

Class Is In Session

INTRODUCTION

I'm not a doctor. I don't have a psychology or sociology degree, but, what prompted me to write this book includes the many relationships I had with woman before marriage, the one I've managed to keep 29 years in marriage, and the fact that during those years, I've been asked, and my wife has been asked by other women to have me teach their sons, boyfriends, husbands, how to be as romantic, passionate, attentive, affectionate, mannish, spontaneous, and in tune with them as they see me with her.

In this book, I will answer their questions and offer this teaching based on things that made me what, why, and how I am in these areas. Besides, I'm approaching middle age, and I feel it's time I passed some of this knowledge along, so that those who can and will use it, have the greatest opportunity to learn the what, whys, and how.

I grew up in a time when love songs were a part of my daily life. From the early 1970's I started listening to and learning the real meaning of romance in relationships, from the lyrics of songs sung by various groups in both pop, r 'n b, and other genres of music. These types of lyrics had a tremendously positive influence on my life, how I treat women, and how I learned what women like and want.

As a disc jockey during most of my teenage years and part of my early adulthood, I picked up on, and immediately noticed how soft music, love songs, and the lyrics from those songs affected the women at those parties. Why and how that is, I learned, is simple. Because every woman was dreaming of and fantasizing about the romance they were listening to in the songs, especially if their boyfriends and husbands weren't measuring up to what was being sung.

That music, and unfortunately its influence, all but died in the mid 90's, replaced with loud, degrading, loveless, types of music that the generation of young people, both boys and girls, gravitated to. I call them the lost generation because most, not all, are lost to the positive and lasting influences they missed from love songs, simply by clamoring and opening their ears to beats and lyrics that do the opposite of teaching them how to love and how to open up to receive love.

One of the other great and possibly the greatest influence on my romantic life was a relationship I had from 1976-78, with an older woman, the sister of a good friend. She was a well-known magazine model around Chicago, and again, was 20 years older than me. Not only did she teach me how to please a woman, but the residual effects of my relationship with her, (i.e. the pats on the back I received from my peers, and the endless invitations I got from girls who previously wouldn't even look my way), gave me the biggest shot of self-esteem I could ever have hoped for. For all it's worth, the relationship with her made me the romantic, attentive, mannish man I am today.

The second greatest shot to my self-esteem was a friendship I had from 1978-83, with a brotha named KC, who became my best friend, even though I have not seen him since then.

He was the coolest dude in my neighborhood.

We became friends instantly.

He was the personification of cool.

All the girls, and women, in our neighborhood knew it and they did everything to be anywhere near him, and he soaked it up, and so did I.

The girls and women he dated, handed me their friends.

The residual effects of me being his best friend, were lasting and lifelong. And, being the DJ at all the house parties, didn't hurt either.

Plus, we didn't dress our age. I don't know where K's ideas came from, but mine came straight from the pages of GQ magazine.

What they wore, I wore.

It got me plenty of attention from girls, ladies, and older women, and I was a sponge and soaked up all the attention, the self-esteem, and the residual relationships that came along with coolness.

Finding your Mr. Right or him finding you is often like gambling against the odds like public lotteries. Most men, are Mr. Everything during the Pre-Sex Stage. Why? Because we're wired to do any and everything you want us to, just right, in order for you to believe that we, are perfect, for you. However, in the vast majority of men, continuing or even remembering the level of romance and activity you experienced from us pre-sex, is nearly impossible to maintain post-sex.

Once you've had sex with your Mr. Right, the conquer is over. The conquest, won. He tends to relax from romance, and focus more on repeating the act of reproduction, "sticking his pole in the hole", and most women will recognize a change almost immediately.

Again, the things he did before you had sex with him, aren't as vital to him after he gets it. It's not intentional. It's how he's wired as a teen. He actually knows better, but what he doesn't know, is the lasting effects that you having sex with him has just had on the part of his being that associates romance with something he places value on.

Before you had sex, being romantic had a stratospheric value to him, because it was the tool he needed to use to woo you into bed. Once sex took place, he tossed the romance tool aside, replaced by his penis, because he feels romance is no longer needed. And, the more sex you give him without requiring him to be romantic, the less value he places on romance. Therefore, over time, he starts to ignore it, and even forget parts of what he learned about even being romantic.

In this book,

Romance 101: Class Is In Session

the Course material is a compilation of research, reality, and recollection. For the list, I used three criteria for coming up with 100 names and definitions that if studied and applied, can help create your own wish list, for your Mr. Right.

REMEMBER: your *Choices*, the *Characteristics* you look for, any *Compromises* you are willing to make, helping to *Conform* his past behavior, and learning about your areas of *Compatibility*, all lead up to a simple *Challenge* to teach your Mr. Right, using the *Concept* of learned behavior and proven strategies, how to be and stay romantic, and also enable you to measure his progress using the *Charts* I've provided.

Enjoy reading the book, because I enjoyed writing it.

REMINDER:

> your *Choices*,
>
> the *Characteristics* you look for,
>
> any *Compromises* you are willing to make,
>
> helping to *Conform* his past behavior,
>
> and learning about your areas of *Compatibility*,

all lead up to a simple *Challenge* to teach your Mr. Right, using the concept of learned behavior and proven strategies, how to be and stay romantic, and enable you to measure his progress using the *Charts* I've outlined in this book.

Keith Hammond

CHAPTER ONE

CHOICES

CHOICES

We can't choose love, but we can choose relationships.

Have you ever asked yourself, "how did I get into this relationship?" Or, "how did I ever end up having feelings for this person?" Or, has someone asked you, "where did you meet that gorgeous man?" The choices we make in our relationships has a significant and often lasting impact on our thoughts, actions, reactions, in various times and stages of our lives. How we deal with, relate to, and walk through these experiences has an even greater impact on whether we survive them, or we let them severely damage or kill off parts of us.

POSITIVE IMPACT

Relationships we choose to have can have a dynamically positive impact on our life. They can affect us for a short time, long time, or even a season. Not a season in the physical sense, but a period of time. Quite often, some relationships have been divinely orchestrated on our behalf, to make us stronger, teach us, test us, and give us experiences, training and knowledge we otherwise may not have had, sought out, or undergone on our own.

Relationships that have a positive effect on our lives are often the ones we want to keep, spend time on, nurture, concentrate on, and end up having for years, unless it has either been designed to end at a certain time; or, an unforeseen circumstance brings separation such as moving to another part or town, another city, or the other person crosses a boundary that we have set as impassible.

With the increasing use of the Internet to maintain contact and communication with others, it's now easier to foster and finish work on relationships we intend to keep with people we feel are important enough to have around.

NEGATIVE IMPACT

Relationships that have a negative impact on us and our lives, seem to effect us more and longer than those with positive undertones. For example, when relationships end badly, whether its with a spouse, lover, loved one, friend, associate, or business partner, we tend to hold on to those feelings longer. Feelings of anger, anguish, hurt, sadness, pain, unforgiveness, guilt, and a host of other pangs that can sometimes go on for years, even decades.

Why do we hold on to stuff for so long? Because relationships that have negative impact on us causes an initial reaction in us, which if not satisfied, the need to react can last, even into the next relationship. Without remedy, there often is no closure. And without closure, grieving continues. And unresolved grief, can cause depression.

When you don't take charge of your emotions and usher in closure from a relationship that had a negative impact on you, your life, and your environment, it goes in the closet along with your emotions, the reality you need to face, and the reactions you need to have in order to release it, and move beyond it. Why? Believe it or not, everything that you put in the closet, no matter how long you leave it there, comes out.

Here's an example.

My mom passed away in 1972. Our relationship was the typical mother-son bond, full of unspoken and unending love. But, when she passed, it was sudden. I was nine years old, knew nothing about death, didn't have time nor did I take time to react, and the lack of closure caused unresolved grief in me that lasted until shortly before the 40th Anniversary of her death. The feelings of anger, uncertainty, hurt, pain, abandonment, and everything on the list, held open a door that I didn't know how to close. That was the door to my closet.

Eight years after her death, and only two years after I regained enough strength to come out of my introverted shell, the same exact, sudden, unexpected thing happened with my dad. He went to the doctor one afternoon, for a scheduled checkup, was admitted to the hospital, and never came home again. I was 17 years old. It was two days before Thanksgiving. I didn't know how to react, and the lack of closure, again, left open a chasm of unresolved grief, that I didn't get relief from until 31 years later.

Thus, it is important to deal with and bring closure to, in whatever way you can, relationships that have any kind of negative impact on our lives. Get back up, get back out there, find a way to deal with it, even if that means therapy, so it doesn't grab you and hold on for dear life, until you're strong enough to shake it off. My relief, and healing, finally came through my relationship with God, in the church.

Relationships that end badly, and without "immediate" closure, can and will take time to heal from. That is why it is extremely important to find a way to start the grieving process, and move toward healing, so you can move forward. Otherwise, we can and will become lax in every single one of our other relationships with people who still look to and depend on us in other areas and for other things.

Giving our thoughts, feelings, attention, and time
to a relationship that ended badly,
affects those around us in more ways than we can ever list.

Let's say you just had a bad breakup with your boyfriend of a few years, and you thought for sure he was the one. He met your friends, and family, knows everyone you care about at work, and you let him into every aspect of your life. He knows your likes and dislikes. And you know all these things about him. He was the first guy that came along that treated you like a queen, swept you off your feet, and after years of rejecting the notion of falling in love, made you believe in and have hope that finally, dreams that you had long since given up on, had resurfaced from the trunk you'd buried them in, and become reality.

You not only started thinking about and even planning a future together, but even entertained thoughts and conversations of having a family. So why did you break up? Most of the time, believe it or not, it's because he crossed a boundary you set up that if even slightly touched, releases a flurry of emotions you never thought you had.

THE BREAKDOWN

In our lives, since as far back as we can remember, we've heard the term, "breakup". But I'm going to shine some light on this term so as you continue reading, you'll hear the actual term that applies instead of this coined phrase.

Relationships don't "break up" they break down. I'll say it again if you didn't get it. *Relationships don't break "up" they break "down".* People may say breakup, as it relates to the separation, or the feeling that "there's no where else to go but up" but relationships that end badly are actually because something in the process of growing together "breaks down'.

It could be communication, trust, truth, fidelity, or a host of other boundaries, but whatever it is that causes the rift, or tear, between the people involved in the relationships, and caused the breakdown, that, should be your focal point for healing. Again, the rift can be caused by some kind of miscommunication, broken trust, or crossing a boundary that you set up as impassible, such as sleeping with your best friend. I'll say it again, people don't breakup, relationships, break down.

Again, people don't breakup, relationships that end badly breakdown, and the people involved separate from one another because the trust or boundary of the person who has been hurt or affected the most, has been crossed or broken. I say this a lot because it helps reinforce the reality that you didn't break up, something cause it to break down.

WHAT TO DO NEXT

Once that boundary is crossed, and the relationship has suffered what I call irreparable damage, meaning no amount of time or energy or focus or prayer or even outside help can fix it, I strongly recommend that you immediately start the process of grieving.

But, in order to do that, you must release the anger, hurt, and frustration that so often prevents us from starting the grieving process.

How?

By taking the anger out on something else. Join the gym, and take the anger out on the fat in your body and the extra pounds that you've been trying to lose for some time.

Don't have any extra pounds? Take up boxing or self-defense. Kicking the crap out of something else, while you focus on him, or beating the stuffing out of a punching bag that you can paste a picture of his face on with a piece of tape, can help.

And if you let it, can do wonders for starting to release the anger.

Releasing the hurt, pain, and anger, is by and large the first and most important step in the healing process.

Whatever method you use or choose to release it, just get it done.

AND THEN

Open the floodgates where your heart is holding on to the grief. Let the tears flow. Tears can and will, (if you don't fight the process), help wash away the pain, hurt, anger and frustration, and allow you to get back up and keep moving, because you have other relationships that will continue to suffer as long as you let that one affect all the others.

I recommend a trip, alone or with another friend of the same sex. Don't get close or push to get closer to someone of the opposite sex just yet, because then you'll end up in nothing but a rebound relationship, which most often will do nothing but add more hurt, pain, anger, frustration, and separation between another relationship.

Because the rebound relationship will most likely be built on nothing more than the feeling that you need someone to understand what you're going through and with that feeling comes a need to be held and with that feeling comes the need for quick gratification, a boundary which, once crossed, will only lead to more hurt, pain, anger, frustration, etc., which starts the entire cycle all over again.

So avoid the rebound relationship at all cost, and avoid the men who will use this time of weakness for you, as a way for them to get laid. Take it from a man who in the early days of my life, looked for women at parties who would just sit in the corner clutching crumples tissues in their hand, because their friend thought it was good for them to 'get out of the house'. I took advantage of these situations more than once.

Again, what you "choose" to do after relationships end badly is based on the choices you'll make in managing the next relationship. And if not managed properly, it can lead to a bunch of bad choices that you can and will end up regretting for years, and end up affecting all your other relationships, if we don't make the right choices. Again, you can't choose love, but you can choose relationships and how to manage them.

BROKEN HEARTS CAN AND DO MEND

When I was in my teens, I fell head over heels in love with a girl named B. We met one summer and immediately started liking each other. That like turned to love. We were inseparable all summer. At the end of the summer, I went looking for her one day, and she was nowhere to be found. I went to her best friend M.W.s house who lived directly behind me. She told me that B was just visiting for the summer. I ran toward B's aunt's house and on the way there, I saw B in the back of a black car, driving away.

I was devastated. I searched for her everywhere. I found her a month later, but her aunt prohibited us from seeing each other. The devastation and hurt lasted for years.

The next time I saw B, she showed up at my house years later and as soon as I opened the door, she kissed me as if we had never been apart. Then she ran back out the door got into a car, and disappeared back out of my life again. The hurt resurfaced and this time it took much, much longer to heal.

The next time I saw her was five years later when I had moved into my own apartment.

I went in a store to get some furniture, and she worked there. We didn't speak. Possibly because my new girlfriend was with me.

But I'll be the first to admit, I was still hurt and didn't know what to say even if she had spoken to me.

I ran into her again weeks later, in the same neighborhood, at a stop-light. I was in my car, and she was with another guy in the car right next to me. The guy she was with had on the exact same hat as I did, and we were driving the exact same car. I remember her laughing as I stared into their car. She knew it was me.

Her laugh, resurfaced the same hurt and devastation I had held on to for all those years I thought she was 'the one'.

These types of relationships, if you don't release the pain, anger, hurt, and frustration, and start the grieving process, you'll never heal. People don't break up, relationships break down. In this case, that breakdown was separation, that took years to get over, and affected every other relationship I had until I healed. Broken hearts, even young ones, can and do mend. But only if you follow the process of releasing the anger, and grieving, in order to heal and move on, but I had to make the choice to do so.

CHAPTER TWO

CHARACTER

CHARACTER

Traits you can live with, and some you shouldn't

In order to understand how to deal with and manage any relationship with a man, women must first understand the character of that man. And in order to understand the character of a man, women need to first understand the simple things that make up that man.

Women are emotional creatures. **Emotions** are based on feelings, Feelings are based on thoughts, Thoughts are based on ideals, Ideals are based on values.

Men are physical creatures. Physics are based on values, Values are based on ideals, Ideals are based on thoughts, Thoughts are based on Feelings, Feelings are based on **Emotions**.

LOOK AT THE ARC

A woman's emotions come first. A man's emotions come last.

[A SIMPLE CHART TO IDENTIFY THE DIFFERENCE BETWEEN MEN AND WOMEN]

THE COMPLETE OPPOSITE OF WOMEN.

In relationships, men are completely opposite of women. This is the reason we rarely understand each other. Men get physical with things we value. The way that physicality is expressed is based on how much value we place on anything. If we love, respect, and treat a woman like a queen it's because we place a very high value on her.

Men protect that which we value. If we degrade you, and treat you like trash it's because we don't see much value in you at all.

The way women get physical in relationships
is based on how much men positively stimulate their emotions
in the relationship.

The way men approach relationships
is based on the value they place on the physical aspect
of the relationship.

Women are hormonal in relationships.
Men are pheromonal in relationship.

Women's emotions are triggered by her heart.
Women's emotions are triggered by how they have been treated.
Women's emotions are triggered by how they want to be treated.
Women's emotions are triggered by how they see others treated.
Women's emotions are triggered by how they should be treated.

None of these come anywhere close to where men's emotions are.

Men's emotions are controlled by his senses.
Men's emotions are controlled by what he sees.
   ~ Face/body/appearance.
Men's emotions are controlled by what he hears.
   ~ To a man, boring conversation equals boring in bed.
Men's emotions are controlled by what he touches.
   ~ If you don't let him touch you, he'll find someone he can.
Men's emotions are controlled by what he smells.
   ~ If you never smell sexy, sex with you won't be his priority.

Men are conquerors.
We see everything we do
as a challenge to get you
to open your legs
so we can conquer
what is between them.

Women are courters.
You want men to do
everything we can
in the challenge of courtship
to trigger the emotion
that opens your legs.

TRAITS YOU CAN LIVE WITH & SOME YOU SHOULDN'T

Traits you can live with and those you shouldn't are the subject of this chapter on character. For example, unless you're willing to spend years praying for, forgiving, and waiting possibly even more years to see the results of your prayers, forming a relationship with and living with a man addicted to substances is probably not a good idea.

However, as I once was, thus I know from personal experience, that my wife was not only willing to pray for me, she did wait years to see the deliverance and change in me, and the results speak for themselves. After 7 years of her prayers, and a lot of tears, on September 12th 1991, at age 28, I was delivered from addiction to the substances I had been in bondage under since I was 15.

I say it's not a good idea to form relationships that you expect to turn into love, marriage, kids and family, with addicts, because unlike me, and a handful of others, I've seen hundreds of men never get delivered from substances and I've witnessed firsthand the destruction their behavior caused their girlfriends, wives, kids, family and nearly every one of their other relationships.

It takes a strong woman to be able to deal with a weak man. Not weak in a sense of strength, but weak to the temptations of this world that are designed to do nothing more than steal, kill and destroy. Thus, unless you are a woman with the inner strength and resilience to stand in the gap and fight for the good you see in that man, pray for him, shed tears for him, protect him, and be patient year after year, while he mistreats you, even bringing other women around you, I encourage you, advise you, counsel you, and write to you, to seek a normal relationship.

So, let's talk about some of the traits you can live with, and a few more of those you shouldn't.

The first trait I recommend you seek in a man that you're hoping to have a lifelong relationship with is **Alpha**.

Before you close the book, let me explain. You don't have to marry a preacher to get a good man. Heck, you don't even need to find a deacon. But you should be looking for someone who is compatible and equally yoked with you in your beliefs.

While you may think I'm crazy for even mentioning this as the primary thing to look for in a man, I know from personal and practical experience that without this, everything else fails.

What this means is that even if you don't have a relationship with God, make sure he does. Why? Because God created man to be the head of the woman.

Aside from all the liberations, causes, rights, etc., man never has and never will lose his given place in God.

If a man does not have a relationship with God, rarely, if ever, does his life turn out the way 'he' plans.

And because his life won't turn out the way he plans, with you by his side, not having a relationship with God in order to pray and help sanctify that man, both of you are quite possibly fighting a losing battle. I'll talk more on this subject in another chapter, so let's move on to the next trait.

Another trait, in the character of a good man, is **Attentive**. Yes, there are many others that you could put before this one, but in my opinion, if the man you're seeking to form a lasting relationship with is not attentive to your needs, keep looking. According to the Dictionary, synonyms for the word attentive are: helpful, thoughtful, considerate, caring, dutiful, conscientious, paying special attention, kind, courteous, polite, devoted, listening carefully. Put these qualities on your wish list for a man, and likely he will turn out to be a great one.

Along with the man you're looking for being Attentive, a word that doesn't quickly or naturally come to mind as one you would normally put on your wish list is **Assiduous.** But you're about to learn why it should be at the top, if not in the top three things on your wish list. If your man is Assiduous, he does not rest until you and your kids and your household, and your family is well taken care of. He's the hard-working, diligent, tireless, industrious, persevering, get up in the morning with the purpose of making ends meet no matter how he's feeling type. So, you can place whatever trait you think is above this one, but if you don't have this one, you may end up not only being the bread winner in the family, it may be a rare thing for him to even bring home the bread, unless you've sent him to the store with the hard earned money from your own purse. Just a thought.

If you'll notice, I hadn't added the word **Attractive** to the list yet. Why? Because I'm of the opinion that good looking doesn't necessarily mean he's a good mate, or that he's good for you. But, for the purpose of what I recommend for your own wish list, being attracted to someone is more than a physical thing, for women it's an emotional one.

If a man has good looks, but opens his mouth and either can't put two sentences together, or talks like he just jumped off the last line of a hope and dream covered rap song, you may want to think again.

Why? Because if you're educated, and he's edumocated, at some point, you're going to get tired of telling yourself, "but he looks sooo good." And the moment a man that has both good looks, and good grammar comes along, your ears and the part of your womanly senses that attract you to a man, are going to perk up to the point that the magnetism that your edumocated man has on you is going to weaken, and you'll find yourself sneaking second glances at the man that is now awakening feelings inside you that you didn't know you had. And when that happens, no amount of good looks is going to win over that which touches your senses in a way that both challenges your intellect and captures your attention. Thus, being attracted to a man has many facets, which I'll cover more about in another chapter, but just let me remind you of an old saying.....................................'all that glitters...'

Let me prove my point with just a little tour on the background bus to the place where you see "glitter marriages".

First, we'll make a stop in Hollywood, the adultery and divorce capital of the entire world. It seems to be almost a common theme that couples in Hollywood that have what the world considers beautiful women, and handsome men, end in divorce most often than anywhere else in the world. And, in less that 7 years. Why? Because quite often 'all that glitters...'

Then let's take a trip into the world of what I call "mogul marriages". The men in these relationships are either at the top of their game in the music industry, or the sports arena.

The women that find a way to slow these men down long enough to grab hold of them and find a place on their schedules to insert a wedding, often end up learning that the lifestyle of someone who has just come from walking across the stage in high school, or dropped out of college early to pursue a pro career, or came straight from da streets of da ghetto, but have just been handed millions of dollars to live their version of the American dream, come to learn very quickly that 'all that glitters...'

Why not marry into glitter or moguldom? Because if you're not willing to live with the lifestyle that comes with the sparkle on the surface, along with the darkness underneath, often represented by other women, scandals, hotels and headlines, you may want to look past the contracts, cars, and castles, in your search for Mr. Right.

More often than not, these days, the wives and girlfriends of these glitter and mogul relationships are ending up with their own contracts, cars, and castles, and often reality TV shows. However, that still does not outweigh the damage clearly seen from the lives of these women after the relationship has broken down and ended in divorce or separation. Nor does it soften the blow of the anger, frustration, and feelings of betrayal heard from the mouths of these women who become stars by association with the glitter and mogul men they marry.

It doesn't matter what the sparkle on the surface looks like, the simple truth is, unless the character of that man has been foundationally developed with the things on your wish list that you know in your heart of hearts make him a good man, all you're likely getting is a boy with money, with the hopes of him becoming a man with maturity. Let me be the first to say it before your friends do, good luck with that.

The character of a man starts from childhood. But most often, those traits that have been instilled by great fathers and/or mothers, are tossed out the window with the receipt of millions that offer open doors to wealth, wine and women...leaving you at square one. Possibly a little better off financially, but no amount of money can heal the heart from a relationship that has broken down and ended badly. The money may buy you lots of things to use as coverings for the scars that lay just beneath the surface, but as I mentioned earlier, emotions that you tuck away in the closet, without closure, have a way of screaming their way out.

Let me include a brief disclaimer and say that all glitter and mogul marriages and relationships DO NOT end badly.

There are some, a few, that have stood the test of time, but if you do the research you'll find that the men in those relationships and marriages are and were mature before they came into wealth.

Money does not and can not buy love and happiness. So if **Affluent** is on your wish list, let me just say that you need to consider categorizing that word first, and I suggest adding to it, a myriad of other traits that help stabilize that which is in the bank, by building a foundation for you in his heart, and for his home. Then, maybe he'll stay there.

Men with character traits built upon a foundation of faith, with walls of maturity, a presence of prayer, a heart of compassion, and a work-ethic, can withstand the temptations that come with lots of money.

TRAITS YOU SHOULDN'T LIVE WITH

Women, don't browbeat your man. If it's a trait within you that you've seen in other women in your family, but don't believe you have it, or are in denial about it, face reality and get help. Why? Because a browbeaten man will live at home with you and the kids for years, but his hopes and dreams and focus will be somewhere else. And eventually, so will he.

Browbeating is nothing more than verbal **Abuse**. And if you're what society calls an independent woman, few women left in this country are going to allow a man to verbally abuse them for long. And they're certainly not going to allow him to become physical with that abuse.

Why? Because the laws have changed that make it easier to lock up a man that does these things, without a woman's complaint, and, there are many great social service agencies that can help as well.

Unless you're willing to follow the golden rule of do unto others, don't do it to him. And you should definitely not allow it to be done to you.

A man that verbally abuses a woman, is already well on his way to physically abusing her. So, if the man you're seeking to have a lasting or long-term relationship with is verbally and/or physically abusive...run. Put on your track shoes, wait until he leaves the house, grab what you can carry, and hit the road Jill, and don't you come back no more...no more...no more...no more. And be careful never to return because situations can escalate and get worse if you do.

When you get to the end of this book, and you make or update your wish list, make sure abuse is on the list of Traits You Don't Want. And by all means, stick to it.

A recent TV talk show chronicled and featured women who are doing time in prison for killing the men that were abusing them.

It also talked with women who are still living with and dealing with the seemingly never-ending cycle of abuse.

And it remembered those who lost their lives waiting and hoping for their men to change, while keeping the abuse a secret from people who loved them.

Relationships with abuse as a part of daily activity, regular routine, or weekend schedule, are not normal.

Women who are being in any way subjected to any type of verbal or physical abuse need to leave and seek help immediately from the authorities and agencies.

There are other signals that the man you're seeking to form a lasting relationship with may be an abuser, so I'll touch briefly on these other character traits as well.

These are in no way all of even close to being all, but here are three.

1. Authoritative (overly dogmatic)

   If all the decisions in your relationship done by him without any regard for your feelings, thoughts, intelligence or input, be careful. This can turn into abuse. Being the head of household is one thing, but 'I'm the king of this castle', played out long ago.

2. Absorbing (holds everything in)

   When you disagree, does he take in everything you say, only to bring it back up again later in an unrelated spat? If so, be careful. Guys, who are sponges, can be time bombs. They hold everything in, but you should realize that it has to come out at some point.

3. Addictive (not trying to change)

   The vast majority of men who are severely and constantly under the influence of substances are often dangerous. In fact, he may not even remember if he slaps you around a bit when he's in a stupor. This is dangerous, not just for you, but children as well.

Forming relationships that you expect to be lasting ones, with the three types of character traits listed above, can lead you into an abusive relationships.

Not always, and not with all men, but research, statistics, police reports, women's shelters, restraining orders, and many other sources show these facts.

My final advice and recommendation in this area, is to seek help.

REMINDER:

> your *Choices*,
>
> the *Characteristics* you look for,
>
> any *Compromises* you are willing to make,
>
> helping to *Conform* his past behavior,
>
> and learning about your areas of *Compatibility*,

all lead up to a simple *Challenge* to teach your Mr. Right, using the concept of learned behavior and proven strategies, how to be and stay romantic, and enable you to measure his progress using the *Charts* I've outlined in this book.

Keith Hammond

CHAPTER THREE

COMPROMISE

COMPROMISE

He has some but not all of what you want in a man

Before I go to deep into this chapter, I want to say to women every-where, that *compromising in any relationship is what 99% of most women do anyway.*

A man will rarely, if ever, have all of what you want, but he will have some of what you need as a foundation to start and work with. Some-times, the standards and ideals on your wish list are set so high, that you miss opportunities to be with good men. So, if you need to keep reading, let's discuss some typical combinations you'll generally find.

SOME THINGS DON'T HAPPEN THE WAY YOU PLAN

28 years ago, my wife and I met, started dating, and made a com-mitment to each other. That commitment has lasted 28 years. But if you ask her what she saw in me, that made her know without a doubt that I was the one, she'll tell you that she saw my face in a dream, long before she ever met me.

The day we met, she was at one end of an apartment building hall-way and I was at the other end, 60 feet away. We both reached for our respective doors at the same time, and a shock of some sort went through each door knob. She looked at me and asked me if I had felt it and I responded that whatever she had done, she needed to keep it down there with her.

When she smiled, I knew.

A week later, the building flooded. We were on the 13th floor, and a pipe burst, causing a layer of ice to form. And the elevator was broken.

I came out of my sister's apartment, and she came out of her mom's house at the same time. Finding out that the elevator was broken, she began whining and complaining that she needed to get to school.

I demanded that she let me take her downstairs, and she commented something to the effect that I wasn't Superman, and I couldn't fly.

Without hesitation, I picked her up on my back, and headed toward the stairwell. I was on a mission to prove I could be her Superman, and anything else she wanted.

With slippery, burgundy penny loafers on, I strapped on my virtual cape, and carried her down 13 flights of icy stairs on my back, so she could get to school.

In spite of the fact that she wouldn't talk to me for the next six months, We've literally been inseparable since June 22nd of that year, and I think I at least proved I have a super power or two when needed.

I've mentioned several times already that you can't choose who to love, but you can choose who to have a relationship with and how to manage that relationship. Ours has been up at times and down at times, but it's a marriage that has lasted 28 years as of this writing.

I say all this to say that in spite of your hopes, dreams, and even the best wish list, meeting your Mr. Right may not happen the way you plan, and may happen in the oddest of places, and the strangest of circumstances. But be watchful, be ready, and most importantly, be open to the opportunity when it knocks, because if you don't answer the door, it, or he, may not come knocking again.

HE HAS THIS BUT DOESN'T HAVE THAT

I opened this chapter by saying that compromise is and always will be the foundation of most relationships. No one on earth is perfect. They may look and act that way when you first meet them, during what I call the 'blinded by beauty stage' but once the dust settles, and time passes, you'll start to see certain nuances and traits you didn't know he had, and it is at that point, that the decision of whether or not you can live with, and eventually marry this person, is often made.

What if he has the looks you want, but doesn't have money? Or, what if he has money, but doesn't have the exact look you want? Or what if your wish list wants him to have a close relationship with his family, but there isn't one? Or, what if your list says he should love his mother, and she turns out to be like Cinderella's step-mom, and he doesn't want anything to do with her, now that he's free from her grip? These things, and many more, make up the "what if he has this but doesn't have that" category.

Are you willing to COMPROMISE?

Do you compromise on honesty?

For example, if he doesn't tell you or embellishes something about his past, is that a deal-breaker?

And which of these are you not willing to tolerate?

Lying, about anything. Lies are lies. No color necessary.

Lusting, which can lead to pursuing, and eventually getting. Remember, men are conquerors.

Loyalty, meaning he throws you under the bus to save his own skin.

Lewdness, or in other words, you hate porn, but there's evidence that he watches it when you aren't around.

The character traits that you are willing to tolerate, is what you're open to compromising for.

And if you compromise, it means you're willing to settle.

I've heard a lot of women say, "I just want a man. I don't care what he looks like, where he comes from, as long as he's a man."

But I am of the opinion that this statement is more for the one night stand, and not for the lasting relationship.

Mr. Ready may not become Mr. Right,
until he's had a chance to develop the characteristics
that you help mold and shape him into.

Most men will tell you that you can't change them. For the most part that's true. But, while you may not be able to change his character, because it was instilled at childhood, you can help mold and shape his current and future behavior. It's perfectly okay to communicate with him that while you are willing to compromise on certain characteristics, you're not willing to tolerate certain behavior.

PRACTICAL PLACES, MANY FACES
Women say that finding a good man is difficult these days. And that finding a great one is even harder. But in spite of what TV, movies, magazines, blogs, books, and other women say, there are still some of each out there. But, finding them is another story. And, where you look is often the greatest hurdle women place in front of themselves, before your search ever gets started.

Where do you find these good men and great men, who are available, without girlfriends, boyfriends or baby mamas on the side, without a prison number tattooed on their forearm, an addiction they can't shake, some form of education, and at least a decent enough job and credit report so that he isn't looking for you to take care of him?

While I could add a whole host of other search criteria to this list let's first talk about getting past the no-nos and talk compromise.

For example, if your wish list says he has to be tall, dark, handsome with an accent, you either need to buy a one way ticket to Italy or France, or start updating your criteria to include Hispanic, Somali, and other tall, dark-haired men with accents.

Again, be hopeful about what you're looking for,
but also practical and specific
about what you want and don't want.

By and large, if you're looking for Mr. Right, just like your wish list that covers his looks and character, you're going to have to create a second list that contains the places you include in your search.

If you're not a bar hop, but he's sitting in a bar surviving on one night stands, and the next round of drinks, check the bar off the list because it's not likely that you'll ever meet him if you don't go in there.

And, if you're into a life of faith and family, and he's never been to church in his life, will you compromise and ask God to point you in the direction of a man, in the church, that has the characteristics and other items on your wish list. However, this is a difficult place these days to search and I'll tell you why. I've been in church leadership for over 15 years, and I've recognized a glaring disparity in the ratio of men to women in attendance on Sunday morning. In smaller churches, with memberships under 500, women outnumber men by 7 to 1. More often than not the larger the church, the ratio becomes equalized.

In the 7 women to 1 man churches, the men that are there are often married, or gay. Rarely will you find a single man sitting in church by himself on Sunday morning, unless he's underage, his mom is still bringing him to church, or he hasn't graduated high school yet. And, there's not much difference in the culture of the church at this number. So if you're looking, but attend a small church good luck with that.

In churches between 500 and 1,000 members, I've noticed more elders, families and settled couples, and again, the numbers are more equalized. Rarely will you find a single man sitting by himself in the pews or attending mass on Sunday morning.

In churches that have been labeled with the title of "mega", where the memberships run into the thousands and tens of thousands, this ratio is often equaled out because of a variety of factors including popularity; the amount of time the church spends doing real ministry work such as reaching out to single men through programs that help them get free of addictions, reintegrate into society from prison, etc. Thus, the equalized ratio of men and women at about 50%.

I've also noticed in various cities around the country that men are the majority of users of services such as homeless shelters, and they make up the majority of prison inmates. Thus, the list of places you search for good/great men may have to include a small notation in margin that asks, "if I meet a man who is/was homeless, or is/was in prison at one time, am I going to still consider him a good or great man?"

If bars, small churches, homeless shelters, and prisons are not on your list of places to search for good men and great men, you've just eliminated a very large percentage of places to search from the list, and an even higher percentage of available good and great men.

But, even if you're not willing to compromise in these areas, there's still hope. If you'll add grocery stores, games, and libraries, you may balance out the number a bit. And, if you compromise on your rule of never ever dating in your workplace, it will increase substantially, because you've just hit the nail on the proverbial head, when it comes to the "must have a job", portion of the wish list criteria.

THE FINEST FRONTIERS
Colleges and Universities, MegaChurches, Sporting Events, and Health clubs, not to mention the increasingly popular online dating sites, are at the top of the list for being the best social environments conducive to helping a relationship get started, and moving forward.

Why?

Because in each of these, there is already something in common. At Colleges and Universities you'll have education in common; At MegaChurches you'll have faith in common; At Sporting Events you'll have love of the game in common; At Health clubs you'll have fitness and health in common; and in online dating sites you'll have searching for Mr. or Mrs. Right in common.

REMEMBER REFERRALS

When trying to find a good man or great man, a referral from someone you know and trust, and who knows and trusts you, is still considered one of the greatest ways to locate Mr. Right. However, in my nearly three decades of experience in a relationship with the same woman, my advice is to always keep your respective families and friends at bay when it comes to your relationship. They are great sources to help you locate Mr. Right, but when you start getting to know him, tell them, politely, to back off.

After I met the woman who has been my wife for 28 years, her brother became my barber. And her other brother became my best friend. But when I met her sisters, and her mom, I later moved my wife 450 miles away, if you get my drift.

MORE WATER FOR THE POOL

Now that we've discussed at least a little about the most popular places to search for or meet Mr. Right, where else could be considered locations to add to your list? Meetings about social causes that you're passionate about or actively involved in, and the Military.

A CLOSING THOUGHT ON COMPROMISING

Compromising can seem a little disheartening until and less you start thinking about the big picture.

The benefits of compromising can be tremendous if you align that with "conforming" in order to help mold and shape his current and future character into your model of Mr. Right.

CHAPTER FOUR

CONFORMING

CONFORMING

You can't change his past, but you can help shape his future

18-25

Men between the ages of 18-25 are by most opinions the ripest fruit in the vineyard. Why? Because they've rarely been unscathed by relationships that broke down; aren't damaged beyond repair from their boys will be boys stage; but you may have to compromise in terms of them being skilled in the art of how to romance, take care of, and please a woman, unless they've spent time on the Internet learning what a clitoris is, how to locate the G-spot, and that there are more places to eat than fast food restaurants. You're less likely to have to worry about their past, but this is prime time to help mold their character into what you want in your Mr. Right.

26-35

Men between 26-35, if they're still single, are often dissatisfied with dating, but still searching for Mrs. Right; distracted with the dynamics of their careers, but still hoping to meet the girl of their dreams; done searching, but keeping one eye open just in case. But, this is the most pliable age group because the richness of your experiences can help the two of you grow together and learn each others ways best.

36-45

Men ages 36-45, if single, are often divorced, or single by choice. Aside from the fact that they are dangerously close to being considered by many women as being over the hill, there's still hope.

However, many women of the same age, if they're still single, are reaching back into the pool for younger, more virile men who are more than happy to make the "cougar connection". So, if you're starting a relationship with someone in this age group, you're less likely to have to mold and shape him into anything, because his life experience will probably be more than sufficient to meet the standards on your wish list.

46-55
Men at this age, if they're still single, I have absolutely no comment about. Nothing to say. No opinion. Not a word.

How do you compromise by conforming? First, it wont be easy because most men I've ever met, befriended, counseled or just talk to either leave me with the impression or outright told me that they would never allow any woman to change them.

When it comes to conforming what your focus should be is to help a man that you want, that has traits or characteristics you don't like, gradually stop or conform to a new or alternate way of doing things. For example, if your man or the one you want has all the qualities on your wish list, but the one major thing you don't like is that he smokes cigarettes, learn ways to help him to stop or try an alternative method to getting the fix he has grown accustomed to from nicotine. How? First, be honest with him and tell him the reasons you don't like his smoking. Whether it be his health, your health, the smell, or the fact that he expects you to kiss him knowing you hate the smell and taste, communicate that.

When you've gotten past the communication stage, do the research and offer him a smokeless, tasteless, alternative to his cancer stick. There are numerous ones on the market that work, and only you can determine which one is going to be the one for him. While it may take a few trials to locate the one that works for him, the end result will likely be a trait that you don't like, conformed into a behavior you can tolerate.

And, your success is in the fact that his smoking wasn't a deal breaker; and you were willing to compromise time, effort, and a little work to help mold and shape his future behavior.

Let's take another one

He's your Mr. Right, but you hate the fact that he flirts. He says it's innocent, but it cuts you to the core because you're supposed to be the only one he gives that type of attention to.

Again, first, communicate to him how it makes you feel. Then, do the research to find ways to help him stop, and you will most likely find that there isn't much out there, but the one sure way to get him to notice his behavior is for you to flirt so that he can see himself in it, and feel a little of what you feel.

Be careful with this because if not done correctly, can spark serious arguments, blame throwing, and often separation between you.

This experiment is not to break down the relationship, it's to help conform his negative behavior so that you can get a positive result.

And yet another one

Let's say your Mr. Right is ideal for you, but he has a tendency to occasionally want to have a night out with the boys, but their locations irk you: bar, club, strip-club, etc.

Why?

Because you know that there are single women at bars, and clubs, a little tipsy, under-dressed, overly flirtatious, and may or may not consider your Mr. Right a hunk of prime man meat, even though he says it's an innocent night out with the boys.

How do you conform his behavior? Again, first, communicate how it makes you feel, and if it doesn't stop, try this. One the night that he has planned to go out with the boys, you start getting dressed as well. Get you hair done. Brush on some makeup. Put on the sexiest dress you can find. Then, follow him to wherever it is he's hanging out with the boys. Only, you're not following him there for him, you are going there to let him see himself through you.

When you get to the bar or club, without letting him see you, just sit back and observe, just what a night out with the boys consists of. When you've seen enough, turn up the heat a bit. Go over to him, plant a kiss on his cheek, tell him to have a good time, then walk away, find a dance partner, and get your groove on. Short of having to take the mace out of your purse to fend off an unwanted advance, only do what it is you have seen him doing. When he comes over to you to ask you if you've lost your mind, and wants you to leave with him, sit him down and ask him if he wants you, or his behavior.

Men in committed relationships need to act like it. And unless you, as his woman, are willing to help conform his behavior by helping him to see how ugly it is, most men won't change.

However, if you are willing to take the time, and help nudge him through an exercise, so that he can understand how serious you are, you may be quite pleased with the results. Then, the next time he comes talking about a night out with the boys, simple take out the dress you wore and lay it on the bed, and see just out quickly he remembers and responds.

Helping to conform a man's behavior isn't changing him. It's simply helping him to correct something he shouldn't be doing anyway. If he starts the argument that he was that way when you met him, and you liked him for who he was, and a man is going to be a man, blah, blah, blah, kindly let him know that if he plans to continue down the road of romance with you, he will either stop doing what he's doing, or hit the road, and go darken someone else's door with that mess.

Structure, respect, and boundaries are a normal part of, and essential elements in any relationship. Once you lose structure, respect or cross a boundary, it is extremely difficult to repair, restore, and heal from.

Men generally don't know what boundaries we can't cross, even if women think they should be obvious. Women give men way too much credit for knowing these things. As men, we use our penises to conquer, so we're not professors of civics. And, if we let our little head do the thinking for us, the big head with the brain will follow.

It's not rocket science ladies, men are physical creatures. Most men are weak to the temptations of beautiful women. And unless he's already strong enough, or been through some effective will-power, or 'reel-him-back-in' exercises that helps him realize that 'you' are the woman of his dreams, these things can and will continue to effect him. It is up to you, as his woman, to recognize his weakness(es) in the relationship, and help to strengthen those areas by using the techniques in this book to help conform any negative behavior into something positive and tolerable.

The vast majority of couples I have witnessed separate over the past 28 years that my wife and I have been together, is because the woman wasn't willing or knowledgeable of the fact that <u>she</u> was the one who needed to take the steps to help him change, rather than waiting on him to do it himself.

Honestly ladies, if you expect a man to stop his learned, and possibly habitual behavior, on his own, without help, good luck with that.

Men are creatures of habit. Once we learn something works, we are not likely to change or alter the behavior, until something helps us change direction, learn, see, and conform to an alternative method.

The formula is simple
An object in motion
will continue on its path
until another object steps in the way.

And sometimes,
you have to be the object that steps in his way!

CHAPTER FIVE

COMPATIBILITY

You say pink he says blue. He says two boys, you say two girls too.

There's an old adage that says opposites attract. Here's some insight that's even older than the adage.

Males are naturally attracted to females, so yes, opposites attract. However, in the broader scheme of things, two people from different backgrounds, cultures, standards, economic status, way of life, viewpoints, can be attracted to each other in a number of ways.

Have you ever seen a couple together and asked yourself, Wow! How did he get her, or OMG! Where did she meet him? Honestly, I did it recently when I saw a Jewish girl hugged up with a Somali boy. What hit me wasn't their cultures, she's what most people would consider a Hollywood beauty, but he's just an average looking kid. They are opposites in every sense of the word, and that very fact may be what drew them to each other.

COMPATIBILITY is the number one reason people give in surveys of how they got together. Looks, is the second reason. Most would think it would be the other way around, but it isn't.

Compatibility plays a hugely important role in the forming and the continuance of a relationship. But, it's not the most important part. Things that you're incompatible about may be what draws you and keeps you together. Your like and dislike of certain things and certain facets or aspects of society or life, may be the very thing needed to keep you communicating, and challenged.

Things such as

Faith	[I like big churches, my wife enjoys small ones]
Family	[my wife likes big families, I'm pretty much a loner]
Politics	[my wife and I are pretty compatible in this area]
Social Causes	[my wife and I are pretty compatible in this area]
Outdoors	[I love outdoor activities, my wife not much at all]
Movies	[my wife and I are pretty compatible in this area]
Music	[I enjoy mostly all music, she's into gospel and rnb]
Sex	[my wife and I are extremely compatible in this area]
Kids	[I'm done raising kids, my wife wants to keep going]
Risk	[I like any challenge, my wife won't take any risk]
Money	[we're compatible, but I'm risk/reward, she's 9-5]
Law	[we both believe the system needs many changes]

Being compatible takes some compromise, but shouldn't affect your core beliefs or your values.

As you'll see in the back of this book, following are the areas that I suggest you seriously test your compatibility level in.

Why?

Because if you're not compatible or connecting in the following areas, but you're looking for or expecting what you already have to be a lasting relationship, it may eventually drive a wedge between you. Here's the short list, but I get more in depth with each topic in this chapter such as how to use differences to your advantage to make your relationship stronger.

Spiritually	Are you of the same belief or faith?
Attractiveness	Are you both equally attractive?
Financially	If this is too lopsided, be careful.
Sexually	Are you both completely satisfied?
Emotionally	Do you cry easier? Does he cry at all?
Sensitively	Are you both sensitive to similar social issues?
Romantically	Are you both romantic? Or is this one sided?
Physically	Do you both enjoy staying fit?
Intellectually	Are you both stimulated and challenged?
Humoristically	Do you tend to laugh at the same things?
Athletically	Do you enjoy the same sports or activities?
Characteristically	Do you both have similar traits?
Communicatively	Do you both open up and talk to each other?
Culturally	Do you both enjoy plays, concerts, etc.?
Creatively	Are you both using your creative side?
Musically	Do you both have similar tastes in music?

These things and many more can make or break relationships.

If one or more of these areas are unbalanced to the point that it swings to far to one side or the other, it can be a deal breaker, or divorce maker.

Find your area of compatibility, learn if you're willing to compromise, and study your man to find out what you see in him that you're not willing to live with, or learn, through a book like this one, what it takes to help him conform his behavior into something you can and are willing to live with.

SPIRITUALLY

Religion plays a significant part in the choosing of a mate. If you're from different religious backgrounds, believe different things, practice different faiths, attend different churches, etc., this almost always drives a wedge between any relationship.

For example, if you're catholic, your probably not going to seek after a baptist, or be comfortable attending a baptist church. And vice versa.

However, couples where the man and woman are both baptists, apostolics, lutherans, methodists; often have no problem marrying or attending the same churches.

It's only when you cross religion in a relationship that problems seem to occur. Such as going from Baptist to Seventh Day Adventist, or Catholic to Jewish, or Muslim to Jehovah's Witness.

And, problems seem to elevate to severe levels when two people with distinctly different religious beliefs, have kids together, because the question of which faith they'll be raised under can draw a line between the relationship. If there's no compromise by the mom or dad, problems persist.

So whatever your foundational aspects faith played, or still cover, know that this is one area that can be supercharged with emotions on both sides, and compromise rarely, if ever, exists.

ATTRACTIVENESS

If you're a beauty queen and he's the unpopular short kid from school; or, if he's the hunk and you're the freckle faced red head girl next door, physical attractiveness can have both positive and negative bearing on your relationship, or who you choose as Mr. Right. And, there are plenty of things you can do to enhance and maintain your looks if you're not considered a beauty queen, or if your Mr. Right isn't quite there yet.

Haircuts or styles that bring out your natural features; visits to the dentist to get a warm and welcoming smile; and a day or two a week at the gym, to take care of your overall physical appearance can do wonders to increase your attractiveness.

Clothing and style are additional options. If you always see him dressed for success, but you're more comfortable in jeans and t-shirts, unless he sees your inner beauty and physical attractiveness, it's unlikely you're going to catch his attention. There are plenty of makeover shows on TV where they give great tips; and a host of salons, consignment shops, and places to get advice on what the latest trends are in attire, but the best thing to do is to learn what he likes.

For example, in order to find out what my wife liked during the six months she wouldn't talk to me, I asked her brother to become my barber, and during those many haircuts, I asked questions and learned all I needed to know. After six months of getting educated by someone who knew her best, I used what I'd learned and she couldn't resist. She thought I was a mind-reader. LOL.

PHYSICALLY

If you're way overweight and rarely exercise, but the man you're attracted to stays in the gym and is solid as rock, and rippled like waves,
it can cause some difficulty if you don't find compatibility in this
area.

I'm not saying encourage him to stop working out, become a couch
potato and gain 150 pounds, but there should be some connection
between the two of you when it comes to your health, especially if
you plan to have children.

Here's one way that your physical differences can be used to your
advantage in building a strong level of compatibility in this area.

Start working out 'together'. At the same time, start fasting (yes, no
food at all for days at a time), and you'll be surprised how rapidly
the weight drops off.

To start a fast, I always try to walk 10-15 miles the first day, to
kickstart my metabolism into eating up the food and fat already
stored in my body, and by the time the 3-day, 5-day, or 100 hour
fast is over, I'm slim, trim, looking and feeling great. And, you can
do the same if you're the one who stays in the gym, but the man
you're attracted to is a couch potato. Help him (by using the same
behavior-changing techniques) to see himself through you. He'll notice if you suddenly stopped exercising and started sitting next to
him on the sofa during your workout times. So find a way to help
him get up off that couch with you!

SOCIALLY

Becoming active in social causes is not only a great way to meet Mr. Right, but also a fantastic way to enhance a relationship you already have.

For example, if the two of you are both touched by the famine you see advertised on TV, then find a local shelter to serve food at; or connect with an organization that packages and sends food overseas to underprivileged countries.

If you're more hands on, there are dozens of reputable organizations (if your church isn't active in this area) that can get you connected with groups that take mission trips where you can volunteer to help in a cause that you're passionate about.

And, it's a great way to spend time together, learn more about each other, and grow together.

And, if you're totally into helping others, start an organization of your own such as sending Bibles in their own languages over to other countries; or eyeglasses and shoes to countries where kids rarely get such items; or connect with a local library or school to start volunteering as tutors.

You'll be surprised at how great your relationship becomes when you have a cause to focus on, work together in, and benefit others with. My wife and I have been actively connected to and involved in our church for over 15 years, and the benefits are immeasurable.

FINANCIALLY

When my wife and I first met, years prior to relocating, I made money with my first construction company. But when we relocated to a new state, we were broke. With two kids to raise, I worked a temp job at night, and my wife volunteered, which turned into a job, which she's still at 19 years later, and she's now the director. Looking back, we're thankful for both hard times and happy times. Both helped us grow.

In several businesses I've started over the years, including some that failed and a couple that landed me in trouble, I made money. However, during tough times when I was unemployed, blacklisted, and couldn't find a job, my wife had to be the breadwinner. For the first time in her life she had to learn how to manage the financial aspects of our household. Over the years, because I took the business risk while she maintained her 9-to-5, we've been through evictions, bankruptcies, foreclosure and a host of other setbacks [*plug for another one of my books http://successaftersetback.com*]. It was understood between us that my finances take care of the family; she used her income to do for herself; and we compromised on the kids. We've lived in everything from a one bedroom apartment, to a half-million dollar house in a gated community, and everything in between.

So, if you're the breadwinner, and your Mr. Right isn't producing any or little finance to help support your relationship right now, pray, and continue to support him until you feel he's had ample time to get there, or to recover. And, if you feel you've done enough to help encourage him to do something to change his situation and help support yours.

However, if your Mr. Right was not work, before you became a couple, you must be willing to compromise and support both of you financially in order for your relationship to work.

That means don't look at him funny when you're on a date for dinner and a movie and he doesn't move to get the tickets or pay the check. But, if he's the breadwinner, and your financial house is in order, that's a great place to start, or grow from.

Be careful if either of your incomes is so lopsided that it causes a rift between you. Relationships can become strained if there is a significant gap between your income levels.

Again, compromise and communicate

A woman who feels she can't depend on her man, may quickly lose interest if she doesn't see a light at the end of the proverbial tunnel. But a woman who sees that her man is just making his way through a rough patch, should remember that in any 'relationship' it takes two to make all things work. And they can work. If you're willing to be committed to it.

If you're not committed, you'll not only look for ways and reasons for it not to work, you'll find them. And there's nothing worse or more damaging to a man's ego, than a woman dumping him because he can't afford to keep her due to his lack of finances. Thus, if his situation is temporary, be patient. If you can't, be prudent and move on.

SEXUALLY

If anyone ever says to you that sex or making love doesn't play a role in your search to find Mr. Right, or in your decision to stay with him once you find him, let me offer some insight.

I've been with the same woman, my wife, 29 years. If you ask her, she'll tell you, "I know her spot". And knowing her spot, has kept me giving her multiple orgasms, including squirting ones, for 22 years.

While I had plenty of knowledge of how to please a woman long before I got married, everything I learned from being with 62 women before marriage, and with my wife all these years, taught me that a woman who is not being satisfied by her man, is by far, the number one or number two reason most relationships break down, and most marriages end in divorce.

Most women will tell you that if a man isn't satisfying her, it doesn't matter what he looks like, how much money he has, or what his status is, she will most likely eventually look elsewhere.

Being compatible in bed, makes a world of difference in any relationship or marriage. And if your Mr. Right isn't in control in bed, ravages you from time to time, able to teach you a thing or two, give you full body baths with his tongue, sucks your toes, tickles every one of your erogenous zones, gives you scalp and body massages that relax you to the point of ripping off your own panties, you may be in serious trouble. And don't go out there spreading your legs until you find the right one!

Why? Because that's considered triffling and nasty no matter how you categorize it or what 'we're just friends' spin you put on it.

As a woman, you may put up with not being sexually satisfied for a little while, but over time, if there's no fulfillment, most women look elsewhere, or move on completely. And yes, I've heard the argument from many women that their 'little battery operated friend' sitting in the drawer next to the bed 'is all she needs'. And others who say, 'as long as I have my pocket rocket I don't need a man.' Quit playin`.

The hard truth is, even a dozen pocket rockets along side a sybian machine is no match for a Mr. Right that knows how to use his hands, lips, tongue, mind, motion, and mannish, to thoroughly satisfy you.

A man that can make your toes curl, and have you giggling uncontrollably from having so many orgasms that you can't even make your own body stop, will make you throw your little friend and the batteries in the trash.

Women who are looking for more than just vibration in this area know the value of a man who offers romance, stability, virility, spontaneity, variety, and experience.

A man who is in control can also teach you to participate at a level that keeps both of you satisfied. And if your Mr. Right is wrong or struggling in this area, and you can't or won't teach him, my advice is to keep teaching, or get ready to become a lonely, unsatisfied, disgruntled, overly emotional, girlfriend or wife.

ROMANTICALLY

Being with the same woman for 29 years, I've learned a thing or two about ways to keep the fire lit.

Any woman who says romance is not important in a relationship or marriage, doesn't know the meaning.

Let me explain, from a man's perspective

First, remember that men are conquerors and women are courters. Romance to a man is divided into two categories:

    (1) Pre-sex romance

    (2) Post-sex romance

In Pre-sex romance, a man is going to give you his absolute best. You're going to see a little of Billy D., Brad P., George C., Richard G., wrapped in the accent of Sean C. He knows a little about everything. He's sensitive to your needs; is a great listener, and communicates.

Without being asked he brings flowers, candy, cards, gifts, takes you to movies, shows, plays, concerts, candlelight dinner, dancing, long walks, romantic weekends, foreplay, is mannish, and cooks for you.

His qualities and senses are heightened to a level that is impossible to maintain over the long-term, because he is in conquer mode.

And once he conquers what you made him wait to get, or you gave in immediately, he no longer has to keep up the charade of being Mr. Everything.

In Post-sex romance, you're going to start to see the real man.

He may be able to keep up the Mr. Everything charade for a few months after you've given him some, but it won't be long before he starts replacing the experience of having to conquer you, with post-sex relaxation mode.

You'll see flowers only on occasion. Candy only on Valentines day. Cards and gifts only on special days and holidays…if he remembers these things at all without being reminded by the media and advertising in the stores.

Movies will be rentals unless it's something he really wants to see. Taking you to shows, plays and concerts will drop off significantly, and forget about long walks or romantic weekends.

Communication will cease. And so will listening. If he likes to, or if you bug him enough, he'll cook for you, but don't look for candlelight unless you strike the match. And dancing, will be a distant memory.

He won't even remember what foreplay is; and his being mannish, will probably only be when he wants quick 'wham bam thank you ma'am, rather than it being a prelude to passion.

Basically, your Mr. Right will have settled into something totally opposite of the level of romance you experienced in the Pre-sex stage, but if you're willing to put in the work, <u>you</u> can help him maintain it.

REMINDER:

      your *Choices*,

      the *Characteristics* you look for,

      any *Compromises* you are willing to make,

      helping to *Conform* his past behavior,

      and learning about your areas of *Compatibility*,

all lead up to a simple *Challenge* to teach your Mr. Right, using the concept of learned behavior and proven strategies, how to be and stay romantic, and enable you to measure his progress using the *Charts* I've outlined in this book.

Keith Hammond

INTELLECTUALLY

There is nothing more embarrassing than if you're at a social gathering with your Mr. Right, and although he may be the most handsome guy in the room, you learn that he can't even hold an intelligent conversation, even when talking about the most basic things.

Okay, so mingling isn't his thing. But that doesn't mean it can't be.

Take classes and learn some things together. Why? It will give you and him things to talk about with other people when you're in situations like that. Next thing you know, his description of how glass is made, or how pottery takes shape on a wheel, or how within 15 minutes, an entire portrait can be painted. Challenge your Mr. Right to keep you intellectually stimulated. And, vice versa. Be creative.

For example, learn a language together just to use it during sex

HUMORISTICALLY

Having a sense of humor helps. If your Mr. Right can keep your funny bone tickled and keep you laughing, it will keep you smiling. Taking time to laugh benefits your heart, the skin on your face, and does wonders for a relationship or marriage. Take a look at the sample Post-Sex Romance Calendar for May, I included a Comedy Show for the 25th. While you can do this anytime, I find it better to schedule it out, make a date of it, so your mind will be ready to see it when the day and time arrives. Laughter is the best medicine for any post-sex romance calendar, so be sure to keep plenty of days to take in fun and comedy.

ATHLETICALLY

When it comes to sports, men tend to be a bit territorial. We know that women rarely take an interest, so while you can give him his time to be away at sporting events with the boys, I encourage you to learn ways to take an interest in sporting events.

There are games available to schedule and go with him to watch all throughout the year, and there are co-ed bowling and softball teams you can join together.

You can take it a step further by learning the terminology on your own, but let him continue to teach you the lay of the land by asking the right questions.

Men are happy to share our knowledge with you as long as we see that you have a sincere interest in hearing what we have to say. Add games and co-ed sports to your calendar, today.

As men, sports are in most of us, by nature. Not all of us, I said most.

If athletics come naturally to your Mr. Right, and it's something he is gung-ho about keeping a part of his life, it's your job, duty, and assignment as his woman to 'encourage' that.

There is nothing worse, than after you two become a couple, than you dogging his wanting to shoot hoops with the fellas, or hit a few home runs for the team, because it helps him, stay healthy, for you. So you, should make the sacrifice, and step aside, for him.

CHARACTERISTICALLY

Do you have the same character traits?

Do you like the same things?

Do you dislike the same things?

Have you ever talked about it?

Why is this even important?

Let me explain the reasons...

The theory that opposites attract may have brought you together, but staying together in a lasting relationship with your Mr. Right takes work. It takes learning each other and it takes communicating what you both like and dislike.

For example, in the calendar exercise I have several days sprinkled where he brings or sends candy to your job.

To a vast majority of men, his first instinct won't be to a thought of what's your favorite candy, it will be to his remembrance of what he does when he's asked to get candy, which will lead him to think about Valentine's day, which will prompt him to buy chocolate.

Now that may be fine, but I'm trying to help you, to help him, learn and understand how to not be mundane and boring, but be creative and unexpected. Meaning, bringing you candy without you having to tell him, remind him, beg him, or prod him.

Again, post-sex, most men actually forget what he used to do for you. But reminding him repeatedly, but gently, will work wonders.

Thus, in a conversation about your likes and dislikes, even if you have to take a note-pad and write it down for each other, if you like dark chocolate, and he show's up with light chocolate, you're going to appreciate the gesture, but start to wonder about how much thought he put into it.

If you like chocolate strawberries, and he never gives them to you, you're going to start wondering if he's really ever listening or paying attention to what you tell him about yourself.

Another example, is when he is supposed to bring or send flowers to your job, if it's never your favorite flower, you'll wonder why not.

Again, it's not about the gesture, it's about how much thought a man puts into the gesture.

Having a conversation about your likes and dislikes, or taking time over breakfast on a Saturday morning to write them down, and discuss them, he will learn much more about you than you could ever expect him to remember, but also giving it to him in a note-pad, helps.

Another example is if you like poems written for you, but he's never written one, you can help him learn how by going to the library or bookstore and giving him a gift of a book of poetry. These simple things will help move your relationship or marriage along into a level of being comfortable with each other's characteristics, and is an added bonus to helping you become more compatible.

COMMUNICATIVELY

There is a list of reasons relationships break down, couples separate and many marriages end in divorce.

~ Number one is money.

~ Number two is sex.

~ Number three is communication.

Before my wife and I got together I often wondered about the arguments I would hear about within my own family between the couples when the wife would say, "he never talks to me." I would always think that was weird, until I got married and experienced it myself.

Once men are past the pre-sex romance stage, and have conquered you, we tend to think that just you having us around is enough. Thus, our lines of communication falter a bit.

Most women are naturally talkative. Most men, just the opposite. As a woman, you can help do something about that. Here's how.

During a moment when you are just relaxing, resting, cuddling, sitting out in the hammock, enjoying breakfast together, pick one topic, and only one topic, and discuss it. It could be current events, or something going on within your family, or a problem you know about with another couple. Most importantly, stick to the topic. Women tend to start a conversation about one thing, but end up talking about 10 other things on your minds, and men have no idea how to keep up or even respond to that, so *stick to the topic*. Strong communication breeds strong and lasting relationships and marriages.

CULTURALLY

This subject within this chapter about Compatibility is not about culture, but "being cultured".

Meaning, do you enjoy plays, concerts, operas, symphony, or taking time to dress up and go see an orchestra?

On your Post-Sex Romance Calendar, keep periodic dates of each of these so that you can grow together in this area.

Your relationship or marriage with Mr. Right will benefit greatly from taking time to enjoy these types of cultural events, and even if you're not into such things, can help you step out of the sweats, jeans and t-shirt world from time to time, and appreciate the experiences of others.

And when you do, enjoy it to the max.

Do research to see what others normally wear to such gatherings.

Dress up. Make a date of it.

The same is true whether you go to a rap or rock concert, or a symphony. Your attire will be adjusted applicably to the occasion.

Being cultured, and growing together culturally, doesn't mean you give up who you are, it just helps each of you grow in another area. If you have children together, they'll appreciate this about you.

CREATIVELY

Using Creativity in your search to find Mr. Right, in your existing relationship to Mr. Right, or in your marriage to Mr. Right, simply takes a little thought.

For example, on the Post-Sex Romance Calendar, you can be creative by adding new, exciting things to the schedule that you've always wanted to do.

If you've never been sight-seeing around your own city, or the next 2 or 3 cities closest to you, make plans to do so. Then, make it happen.

Relationships and marriages post-sex, can become settled and start to feel a little monotonous, but it doesn't have to.

There are endless lists of events to see, things to do, shows to attend, places to go, activities to get involved in, and stuff to learn. In fact, if you spread them out enough, and take breaks when needed just to relax, you'll never run out of new things to do and challenge your ability to be creative.

If you're honest, answer these question: Have you...
- taken a dance lesson or dance class?
- visited the states to the north, south, east and west of you?
- taken a class together to learn something new?
- learned a language specifically for foreplay and bed-bouncing?

Why not?

Turn off the TV, grab your keys, and get moving.

There is a world of exciting possibilities out there just waiting for you to get involved, get active, and the amount of creativity you can bring to the table, learn when you get there, and discover together, can keep the fire lit in your relationship or marriage to Mr. Right for decades to come.

The secret is simple.

Rotate the calendar every three months and change the focus of the activity to keep things fresh.

Changing the focus is simple.

If your activity for a certain day in the month is to take a dance lesson, take samba one month, ballroom when it comes around again. If your activity is to take a class together, take pottery one month, then glass blowing when it comes around again.

If your activity is to learn a language together, keep changing languages until you've learned enough to please your own palates and to please your mate, before, during and after sex as foreplay and make a point to only use that language every now and then to spice it up a bit when the bed-bouncing begins!

Whatever you do, make it exciting, keep it fresh, and your Mr. Right will love to be involved, keep active, and stay romantic. Remember, it takes two to tango, but it only takes one of you to grab the keys, and pull the other one along.

MUSICALLY

Music can help keep your relationship or marriage to Mr. Right lively and upbeat in a number of ways. It can also help you find Mr. Right.

Let me explain.

If your wish list includes a notation that your Mr. Right needs to be a musician, then maybe you need to be buying tickets to the symphony, spending an evening in a jazz club, or you can get as extreme as volunteering to do something free, such as marketing, for your favorite band, if you think your Mr. Right is a member.

Once you've found him, keep that Post-Sex Calendar full of excitement. Go dancing, take a music class together, or learn to play an instrument. There are a number of ways that the two of you can stoke the fire once it's lit.

Also, you can discuss your taste in music. If the two of you are compatible in this area already, then you'll have no problem spending a quiet evening just relaxing on the sofa, listening to your favorite tunes, taking time to slow dance or get your hustle on. These things help in a relationship or marriage, if you're open and willing to let it.

If you're not compatible in this area, it's not difficult to get there, maybe not even all the way there, but close enough. For example, if you are into pop and alternative music, and all he wants to listen to is hip hop, and rap, take time to work at finding a common ground in this area.

Make the sacrifice to attend each other's concerts of his favorite group, and schedule the same for him to support your favorite group.

If you're into nothing but gospel music, and he's into nothing but jazz or R n' B, again, attend each other's concerts, or make the sacrifice and spend a quiet evening, queueing up one of your songs, then one of his, then one of yours, then one of his, until you both come to a point of mutual respect for each other's music tastes.

Compatibility that is not already there,
simply needs a little sacrifice and work to help it get there.

You don't have to crossover into each other's genre, but you can certainly love your Mr. Right enough to be willing to respect the differences between you.

Happy listening!

RECAP

All the other chapters was just to get you to this point.
Everything I've said before this was FANTASTIC,
and you'll be able to use the material for many years to come,
but this is where the real work begins.

This is where you turn into the teacher,
and him the student.

Where you teach learned behavior,
and he learns it.

CHAPTER SIX

THE CHALLENGE
AND THE COURSE

THE CHALLENGE AND THE COURSE

Does he motivate, inspire, attract, and excite you?
Great. Here's how to keep it that way!

If you're looking for Mr. Right, the challenge to find him takes work. Or, you can just not look, and hope he finds you. But if you're being proactive about it, and using your wish list to put yourself in the places and paths that you believe he will be at, or eventually cross, then the only challenge is getting there and being patient.

If you've found Mr. Right, or he found you, and your relationship is ideal, including romance, you don't need this book. But in case you hit a snag at some point, for example, if you start seeing the Post-Sex Romance decline, then take a chance and utilize the methods outlined in these chapters to help your Mr. Right continue his pre-sex behavior, and treat you like he did when you first met.

If you're married to Mr. Right, and your marriage has hit a snag, create a Romance Calendar, sit down with him, and ask him to be willing to make the sacrifice to try something new. It's a challenge in any relationship or marriage to keep the fire lit, to keep each other motivated, inspired, attracted, and excited. Many relationships break down and marriages end in divorce because the couple wasn't willing to make the sacrifice to put in the work needed to keep things fresh.

It's easy to blame each other for the problems, let the flame die, and the relationship or marriage settle into a place where the grass looks greener on the other side.

Relationships and marriages take work.

They need to be nurtured in order to grow, and they need to be managed in order to make it. And, it takes both of you working at it, to make it wonderful. If your relationship is worth having, you'll find ways to keep it that way.

As the Mrs. Right in the relationship or marriage, because of the way that the vast majority of men are wired, "you" have to be the one to step into the teacher's shoes, the secretary's shoes, the marketing exec's shoes, the salesperson's shoes, to help keep him on track. It doesn't take much, and it can be done, but in order for you to keep what you searched for, and worked hard to get, you have to be willing to meet the challenge head on and do the work.

Maybe you didn't catch or hear what I just said. If you're the typical woman of the now, you have dozens of pairs of shoes in your closet. So, teach yourself to associate one of your favorite pair of shoes to each one of these activities. For example, when you need to be the sex kitten, put on the red velvet pumps so you can look and feel that way. When you need to sell him on something, black patent leather. Time to be simple but seductive? Get out the sandles that strap and tie halfway up your calf. You get the picture! Besides, what did you actually think all those shows you buy are for? Mix it up a bit. Put your Ms. Right hat on, be creative, and get to work.

Let's discuss some of the things that the vast majority of men have some degree of difficulty maintaining Post-Sex.

First, any man that has a pole can learn to stick it in the hole. That's not the problem. The problem is simple: Once he's been inside the hole once, all he's wired to do is want to do it again, and again.

Thus, the challenge, if you are willing to accept it, (yes, it sounds like mission impossible, but really it's not) is to keep romance, before and in addition to sticking his pole in the hole, on his mind.

It's quite simple actually. It's a list. And, it contains some or all the things he did to get you. Why is it needed? Because now that he has you, his mind is wired to make him believe that his conquest is over, so he no longer has to perform at the level he did during the Pre-Sex Romance stage.

Your challenge, again, if you're willing to accept it, is to conform his mind, with a little work, prompting, and direction, from you, to the point that he is willing to do these things without being asked, prompted, or outright told.

Have you ever said to yourself,

> **"My man would be perfect if he would just**
> _____ **"**

What would you fill in the blank with? Would it be any or all or most of the items listed below? If so, I'm going to teach you, how to teach him, so you can fill in the blank. Again, it's a list. So, here we go...

THE ROMANCE LIST

- Cuddle With Me
- Spoon With Me
- Say I Love You
- Take a Long Walk With Me
- Open Doors For Me
- Kiss Me Passionately
- Hold My Hand
- Make Me Laugh
- Touch Me Sensually
- Be Mannish (Flirt) With Me
- Nustle My Neck
- Lick My Ears and E-Zones
- Fix Me Hot Baths
- Give Me Body & Scalp Massages
- Tongue Only Sex Me
- Give Me Foot Rubs & Toe Sucking
- Pay Attention To Me
- Communicate & Listen To Me
- Candlelight Dine Me
- Flowers, Cards, Gifts, Candy, Poetry
- Weekend Getaways
- Silently Stare Deeply into My Eyes
- Dance Lessons
- Take Classes and Learn Together

Did I miss something? Okay...add it to the list, and the most important part, is to post this list, next to the calendar, on the refrigerator!

Looking at the list, you, as a woman, see these things as being natural. But to a man, most of what he's already thinking without saying it is, "I don't want to have to go back to school just to get sex!"

The truth is, that's exactly what needs to happen.

Here's a basic rule, fact, truth, or whatever you want to call it: MEN RARELY, IF EVER, DO ANYTHING WITH A WOMAN THEY'RE ATTRACTED TO, OR IN A RELATIONSHIP WITH, OR MARRIED TO, WITHOUT HAVING SEX IN MIND.

As a woman looking for Mr. Right, in a relationship with Mr. Right, or if you're married to Mr. Right, the same thing applies. Your challenge, if you're willing to accept it, is to simply use this information to your advantage, which if done correctly, will benefit you both. How? Simple. I want you to remember these words:

LEARNED BEHAVIOR

These are the two words that are going to get, keep and make Mr. Right an expert at Post-Sex Romance. And, he will stay there, but only if you help him.

The vast majority of men are not wired to continue being romantic after the conquest is over. If they were, there would be fewer relationships that break down, and marriages that end in divorce. If I'm wrong, I'll apologize now, but the fact that I know I'm right, lets me continue writing so that women who understand this statement, can get the help they need, to help the men they want.

Again, he's not wired that way, so, you as his woman have to help.

Learned Behavior is not a new concept. It's used in every school, training program, employer, and most facets of society.

It's a proven concept. And, the benefit is amazing:

PRACTICE MAKES PRECISE

Men are not monkeys, but sometimes we act like it. We can be a married man with two kids and a good woman, but the first short skirt and v-neck blouse showing a little flesh that crosses our path, can distract and lead us away as if you don't exist.

But, using the **learned behavior** method, you can help him learn to ignore, avoid, and look the other way when tempted or even tested.

To most men, having an orgasm is like winning the lottery over and over and over again. It's a prize to most of us. And our thinking leads us to believe that all we have to do is buy the lottery ticket (dinner, movie, etc) to increase our odds of receiving the prize!

And, here's some insider information.
When you give us the prize without making us buy the ticket, or basically free, most of us don't feel we need to spend the money (time, effort, etc.) to buy it, ever again!

How's that for learned behavior!
And you, Ms. Right, taught it to us!

Women need to take the 'you do this', 'I'll do that' approach.

Man's need to be romantic is eliminated if women give sex anyway. Thus, women play a major role in men not being romantic. Not that it's your fault by any means. But once you understand how a man thinks, if you keep giving sex without requiring romance, you're actually condoning and promoting our romanceless behavior. And the more you condone it, the worse it gets. Even to the point that if you give us sex without requiring romance, for years, most men will eventually lose the desire to be romantic, and many even forget how.

That's where LEARNED BEHAVIOR, and you, come in.

Men are Conquerors. Women are Courters.

Men want sex. Women want romance plus sex.

An age old problem that women have had the solution to all along. So, let's get to work helping your Mr. Right learn what it takes to be and stay romantic beyond the Courting, Pre-Sex, and Conquer stages.

The first and most important thing is that you remember with learned behavior YOU are the teacher, HE is the student.

Your Course Title is: ROMANCE 101

Your Curriculum is: THE ROMANCE LIST

Your Textbook is: THE ROMANCE CALENDAR

Your Cliff Notes are: CHEAT SHEETS (NOTES, CARDS)

Your assignment as the instructor, is to teach your student how to learn certain behaviors that once mastered, will graduate him to the true "status" of Mr. Right, rather than just the title of Mr. Right.

Everything we do from childhood is **learned behavior**.

We learn how to do our ABC's, we learn how to potty on the toilet, we learn how to do our jobs, we learn how to act or react to just about any situation by watching the behavior of others in the same or similar situation. But through all the training we received from childhood well into our adulthood, there's one course that's never taught...**Romance 101**.

In junior high we are never sent to any romance class, we are taught sex education. Girls are sitting in the class saying eewww. Boys are sitting in the same class with hard-ons. And from that moment, boys become conquer-minded, and any thought of post-sex romance goes out the window. The same boys become men with the same mindset.

For decades, and possibly centuries, or at least since the onset of romantic movies, women have wanted their men to act like the actors they watch on TV and on the big screen, which is the scripted version of Mr. Right, both in title, and in status.

Here's some understanding. During the Pre-Sex stage, most men "are" those actors. They know, and do, all the things you want them to, and they do it without being asked, or told.

However, once you've slept with him, romance becomes unimportant and even the vast majority of men don't understand why. So, why are men nice and wonderful during the Courting and Pre-Sex stage? **<u>Learned behavior</u>.**

From adolescence, boys learn what to do to get a girl, but the critical relationship training stops at that point, and no one ever teaches us how to keep a woman once we become men.

Getting a woman was the main focus. And many men think of it as a challenge; getting from first base to second, second to third, third to home plate. But whatever you want to call it, the premise and purpose for a man is still the same: divide your legs and conquer.

Once conquered, unless there is some additional training for how to keep up the romance beyond the conquest, it stops cold, the flame gets smaller and smaller, the relationship often breaks down and the marriage ends in divorce. And, both the man and woman are left to either wonder why or blame one another.

The vast majority of the blame is often placed in the man's lap, even if women cheat, because she feels that he didn't do enough to keep her after the conquest. When in fact, she is equally to blame for not teaching him how.

That's right, I said it.

Women are equally responsible when 'your' relationships break down due to 'your' man not being romantic. How? Easy. Most men, unless they are 'taught' by a woman, has no clue about what foreplay is. That's the bottom part. The middle, the same is true for romance. The top part, is that most men, unless they are 'taught' by a woman, have no idea what an orgasm is and let me not even say 'multiple'.

Women wanted and fought for equal rights. What you weren't told is that it also means equal responsibility, especially in relationships and marriages to men. So, if your man isn't fulfilling his 50% of the Mr. Right duties, the 50% of your Mrs. Right duties should kick in and help him (1) recognize that fact and, (2) learn how.

~ Men are often saying we don't understand women.
~ Women are often saying that men have no clue.

~ Men are often saying we don't know what a woman wants.
~ Women often say she wants the same thing you did to get her.

Look at the above statement: *"Men are often saying we don't know what a woman wants"*. Men are telling you right in this statement that we need help; that we need retraining, cross-training, to go back to school, refresher course in this area, etc.

Look at some of the many ways Learned Behavior has been a major part of our lives, except when it comes to romance in relationships:
- we learn how to walk
- we learn how to talk
- we learn how to eat
- we learn how to use the toilet
- we learn how to exercise
- we learn how to do our jobs
- we learn how to drive
- we learn how to cook
- we learn how to play sports
- we learn how to have sex

This is all <u>learned behavior</u>. We just need to add romance to the list.

No matter what we want to do, plan to do, hope to do, dream to do, in life, we have to come by it through the training and teaching of learned behavior.

In junior or senior high school, before Reality TV made it cool for a man to be in the kitchen cooking, a boy wouldn't be caught dead in a Home Economics class.

But for the purpose of making boys into better men, it should be a requirement.

And,
Romance 101 should be added to every Sex-Ed Curriculum.

Sex-Ed classes taught us the basics of reproduction,
but nothing about romance.

Women who are teachers of Sex-Ed should be ashamed and held responsible for not teaching the fact that *before reproduction, comes romance.* How's that for equal rights!

Again, female Sex-Education teachers all over this country should be held responsible for the countless relationships that broke down, and marriages that ended in divorce, simply because they didn't teach the art of romance "before" the act of reproduction.

I don't hold the male teachers responsible because one can only teach what one has "learned".

Here's the Problem:

From Sex-Ed classes, boys are taught, that the pole goes in the hole, thereby being wired from that moment on. So later in life when lonely, unfulfilled, unsatisfied women communicate with a man by holding up a sign that says kissing, the man holds up a sign that says pole in the hole. The same is true if a woman holds up another sign that says cuddling; the man is still holding the same sign! Because of this faulty wiring from Sex-Ed classes, the boy who is now a man, has learned one thing; so his sign never changes because that's what he learned. You say talk. He says sex. You say hot bath. He says sex.

Here's the Solution:

If you make romance a "PREREQUISITE" (required course) before letting boys in Sex-Ed, boys, and men, will start to get the message: **the art of romance comes before the act of reproduction** and is equally as important as reproduction. Then and only then will the faulty, decades old Sex-Ed teaching of 'pole in the hole first' will be corrected. And, learned behavior will have the opportunity to do its job to help prevent relationships from breaking down, and marriages from ending in divorce.

ANALYSIS

Society believes if a man is romantic by nature, it's because of one of two things: (1) He has more female chromosomes than other men, and he simply keeps it hidden and under control because it's his secret weapon. *In a recent movie a man could read women's minds. He kept it hidden, used it to his advantage, benefitted from it greatly, all because it was his secret weapon. But, even in the movie, until he "learned" how to use the secret weapon effectively, it was useless to him. Men must learn that sex without romance is useless.*
(2) He has some magic potion or a large penis. But the reality is that he's simply mastered the art of romance through learned behavior.

HOW TO HELP HIM STAY ROMANTIC POST-SEX

As his woman, there are a list of things "you" need to do to help your Mr. Right continue to be your Mr. Everything once he's conquered that sweet spot between your legs for the first time.

When professional athletes prepare for any game, there are certain things they do to stay in the best shape possible:

- they have a training regimen
- they keep a schedule
- they maintain strict diet and exercise

The same is true for any relationship or marriage. I tell men, "The same things you did to get her, are the same things you need to do to keep her."

Relationships and marriages post-sex, tend to settle. But they don't have to. Women still want to be treated like they were during the courting stage. Men, once they've passed the courting stage, and conquered you, just want to keep reliving the conquer experience.

Remember the golden rule...?

Do unto others as you would have them do unto you.

Here's how you, as a woman, can use it to help your man keep doing the things it took to get you. It's really quite simple. Using the do unto others method, when you're thinking about receiving flowers from him, give flowers to him instead. The same for candy, gifts, cards, movies, candlelight dinners, hot baths, dancing, etc. YOU BE THE ONE TO INITIATE THESE THINGS SHOULD REMIND HIM TO THE POINT OF FORCING HIMSELF TO REMEMBER.

It's not a game, it's simply another way of helping to mold and shape the pre-sex behavior that it took to get you, into future behavior that becomes a regimen, and schedule.

Now, let's take it one step further. One the next three pages, I've put together a sample calendar for your convenience.

The calendar can help you help your Mr. Right continue to romance you the way he did during the pre-sex stage.

The calendar is for three months. I suggest doing one for the entire year. Post it on the refrigerator and anywhere you know he'll see it.

If you want to really stay on top of it, go a step further, and during the pre-sex romance stage, *write down*, on another calendar, *every single romantic thing that your Mr. Right does*, then you'll have the info needed to make the same calendar for the next year.

Try it. It works.

Maybe I need to repeat that...

If you want to really stay on top of it, go a step further, and during the pre-sex romance stage, write down, on another calendar, every single romantic thing that your Mr. Right does, then you'll have the info needed to make the same calendar for the post-sex stage. Try it. It works.

THE POST-SEX ROMANCE CALENDAR

During the pre-sex stage, your Mr. Right did everything right. Again, without help, it's literally impossible for any man to keep up the charade of being Mr. Everything once he's conquered you, because the vast majority of men are not wired that way. Men are conquerors. And once he's conquered you, he doesn't see the need to have to keep romancing you. Don't expect him to do these things on his own. It's up to you, as his woman, to remind him and help him remember why it's important. Here's a sample post-sex romance calendar:

MARCH

Sunday	Monday	Tuesday	Wednesday	Thursday	Friday	Saturday
				1 Phone Call in the a.m. Candlelight Dinner p.m.	**2** Phone Call in the a.m. Movie p.m.	**3** Long walk on the beach and Single Rose
4 Church and laundry a.m. Phone call p.m.	**5** Massage and foot rub and sex p.m.	**6** Phone Call a.m. See a play p.m.	**7** Phone call a.m. Volunteer p.m.	**8** Phone call a.m. Movie p.m.	**9** Fresh flowers to your job Sex p.m.	**10** Picnic in the park a.m. Window Shop p.m.
11 Church and laundry a.m. Phone call p.m.	**12** Scalp Massage and hair wash p.m.	**13** Phone Call a.m. Sex p.m.	**14** Volunteer a.m. Phone Call p.m.	**15** Sex & Breakfast a.m. Movie p.m.	**16** Candy & gift to your job Candlelight Dinner p.m.	**17** Phone call a.m. Phone Call p.m.
18 Church and laundry a.m. Ice Cream Date p.m.	**19** Massage and foot rub and tongue only sex early a.m.	**20** Phone Call a.m. See a play p.m.	**21** Phone call a.m. Volunteer p.m.	**22** Phone call a.m. Movie p.m.	**23** Fresh flowers to your job Phone Call p.m.	**24** Watch sunrise a.m. Sex and Dinner p.m.
25 Church and laundry a.m. Phone call p.m.	**26** Massage and hair wash p.m.	**27** Phone Call a.m. Ice Cream Date p.m.	**28** Volunteer a.m. Phone Call p.m.	**29** Phone Call a.m. Cook Dinner Together p.m.	**30** Drive or Fly 3 hours for a sexy, hot tub, romantic weekend getaway..	**31**

THE POST-SEX ROMANCE CALENDAR

NOTICE THE CHANGE IN ACTIVITY THIS MONTH. THIS IS SO THAT YOUR TIME TOGETHER DOESN'T BECOME BORING AND MUNDANE. MIX IT UP A BIT. BE CREATIVE. BUT STICK TO THE CALENDAR. IT WILL HELP HIM LEARN THE IMPORTANCE OF KEEPING THE FIRE LIT IN YOUR RELATIONSHIP.

APRIL

Sunday	Monday	Tuesday	Wednesday	Thursday	Friday	Saturday
1 Return from romantic weekend getaway. Rest.	**2** Call a.m. Cuddle, rest and listen to music p.m.	**3** Call a.m. Light exercise together p.m.	**4** Call a.m. Volunteer p.m.	**5** Breakfast a.m. Candlelight Dinner p.m.	**6** Spa treatments a.m. Concert p.m.	**7** Sex on the beach and Single Rose
8 Church and laundry a.m. Phone call p.m.	**9** Massage and foot rub and sex p.m.	**10** Call a.m. Dance lesson p.m.	**11** Call a.m. Volunteer p.m.	**12** Call a.m. Skating p.m.	**13** Fresh flowers to your job Tongue Sex p.m.	**14** Picnic in the park a.m. Window Shop p.m.
15 Church and laundry a.m. Phone call p.m.	**16** Scalp Massage and hair wash p.m.	**17** Call a.m. Heavy exercise together p.m.	**18** Volunteer a.m. Phone Call p.m.	**19** Sex & Breakfast a.m. Movie p.m.	**20** Candy & gift to your job Candlelight Dinner p.m.	**21** Phone call a.m. Phone Call p.m.
22 Church and laundry a.m. Ice Cream Date p.m.	**23** Swim together a.m. Concert p.m.	**24** Phone Call a.m. Dance lesson p.m.	**25** Phone call a.m. Volunteer p.m.	**26** Phone call a.m. See a play p.m.	**27** Fresh flowers to your job Skating p.m.	**28** Watch sunrise a.m. Sex and Dinner p.m.
29 Church and laundry a.m. Cuddle, rest and listen to music p.m.	**30** Massage and hot tub sex at a hotel p.m.					

THE POST-SEX ROMANCE CALENDAR

ACTIVITY THIS MONTH INCLUDES FRIENDS/FAMILY. DON'T FORGET TO ADD DAYS HERE AND THERE WHERE YOU DO SOME NICE THINGS FOR HIM. REMEMBER, YOUR GOAL IS SIMPLE. HELP HIM TO MAKE POST-SEX ROMANCE A REGULARLY SCHEDULED THING. ROTATE YOUR ACTIVITIES EVERY THREE MONTHS.

MAY

Sunday	Monday	Tuesday	Wednesday	Thursday	Friday	Saturday
		1 Lunch at Noon / Light exercise together p.m.	**2** Phone call a.m. / Volunteer p.m.	**3** Call a.m. / Call p.m.	**4** Drive or Fly 3 hours for a sexy, hot tub, romantic weekend getaway..	**5**
6 Return from weekend getaway Cuddle and rest.	**7** Hot bath, Massage and foot rub p.m.	**8** Call a.m. / Dance lesson p.m.	**9** Phone call a.m. / Volunteer p.m.	**10** Phone call a.m. / Movie p.m.	**11** Flowers to your job a.m. Zoo in the afternoon Sex p.m.	**12** Mini-golf & Carnival with friends & family all day
13 Church and laundry a.m. / Phone call p.m.	**14** Scalp Massage and hair wash p.m.	**15** Lunch Noon / Heavy exercise and Sex p.m.	**16** Volunteer a.m. / Phone Call p.m.	**17** Sex & Breakfast a.m. / See a game p.m.	**18** Candy & gift to your job / Candlelight Dinner p.m.	**19** Attend a wedding / Long walk p.m.
20 Church and laundry a.m. / Ice Cream Date p.m.	**21** Spa treatments a.m. / Tongue only sex p.m.	**22** Phone Call a.m. / Dance lesson p.m.	**23** Phone call a.m. / Volunteer p.m.	**24** Phone call a.m. / Phone Call p.m.	**25** Fresh flowers to your job / Comedy Show p.m.	**26** Host a Bar-B-Que with family & friends all day
27 Church and laundry a.m. / Sex and Cuddling p.m.	**28** Massage and hair wash p.m.	**29** Phone Call a.m. / Ice Cream Date p.m.	**30** Volunteer a.m. / Phone Call p.m.	**31** Phone Call a.m. / Cook Dinner Together p.m.		

Most men are of the mindset that if he gets sex without romance, why does he need to give you romance if he's getting sex anyway?

The only way to teach this answer, so that it sticks in a man's mind, is to do it through learned behavior.

If your behavior, as his woman, is to stop giving him sex until he learns to be romantic, he will learn to be romantic in order to get sex. Help your Mr. Right understand that if he gets the romance right, he won't have to initiate sex, you'll be bringing him the sign that says, 'stick the pole in the hole.'

Here's how potent sex is to a man

If a woman was on the top floor of a skyscraper, with no elevator, laying on a bed with open legs, waiting for him to climb the stairs up to her, but along the way he has to master one task per floor, such as kissing, massages, cuddling, in order to be given the key to the next floor, he would master them without thinking, in order to reach her.

So, again, Mrs. Right, your challenge, if you're willing to accept it, is to **teach the learned behavior of how to be romantic**, to your Mr. Right through the use of notes, calendars, and communication.

Now that you know Learned Behavior has been the missing link in the tie that binds relationships and marriages together, let's talk a little about each of the components, facets, and areas of romance that men need to learn from scratch, or be given a refresher course on:

CUDDLING

Yes. The first one on the list right out of the gate.

Teaching a man how to cuddle so that he does it over and over again, without being prompted, asked, or outright told, is simple.

Again, through the use of notes, the calendar you should now have on your fridge, and other subtle ways of communicating it until he does it on his own, starts by placing it on the calendar at every place you've placed the word sex.

You want him to associate the word cuddling with the word sex, so that he knows the two go together, and that you "expect" it after sex.

Then, taking it one step further, on the day you have sex scheduled, leave him a note saying,
"Good Morning Lover,
I look forward to just laying in your arms
after you've made love to me tonight."

These simple tasks will help him through the proven concepts of:
~ ***word association***
~ ***the art of seduction***
~ ***positive reinforcement***
~ ***learned behavior***

4 ways to teach Romance 101 without leaving home. Now that you understand how to be the teacher in this situation...let's continue.

HOLDING YOU

Cuddling and holding are similar actions, but you should teach them to your Mr. Right by associating them with different times.

For example, when you are experiencing the effects of your monthly cycle, and you just want to be held for comfort, leave him a note saying...

> *"Dear, I'm a little under the weather*
> *but I look forward to just laying in your arms*
> *while we watch one of your favorite movies tonight."*

What you've just done is let him know that you're not feeling well, but you've also involved him in the process by allowing him to do something he wants, and the bottom line is you get what you want, which is to be held.

After a few months of doing this during your cycle, your Mr. Right should begin to associate your cycle with comforting you.

Getting him to hold you without wanting sex is the end zone here. And when he associates your cycle with being able do something 'he' wants to do, without hearing you griping about it, it's a score and touchdown for him!

You've given him victory without even playing the game. And I wouldn't be surprised if he starts thinking on his own by also bringing you a hot water bottle. Enjoy!

SAYING I LOVE YOU

Every woman wants to hear these words coming from her Mr. Right. Most men, even if they are truly in love with the women they are in a relationship with or married to, still have difficulty saying them.

These words have a broad scope and a profound meaning, if they are used in a way and method and moment, that gets their point across. Teaching your Mr. Right to say them willingly, without pressure, takes some coaxing, and coaching, but it can be done. You have to help him understand how important it is to you to hear it, and in what context or situation or circumstance or moment or place or setting you want to hear it. And you'll do this by saying it to him, but through different ways of communicating it.

Example: To start the week off, leave a card for him to say thank you for something he did great the week before.

"Honey, I truly appreciate you for making dinner for me
last Friday night.
I enjoyed the time we spent together."

Then, sign the card with your initials, nickname, or pet name, and a simple, *"I Love You"*. Another example, get a small card, and write something that you know he's looking forward to doing in a week or so, *"My Sweet, I'm looking forward to helping you take time to host a bar-b-que for your family. It means a lot."* Sign it, *"I Love You."* Put it in an envelope, put a stamp on it, address it to his job, and mail it. Subtle ways to start getting him to associate the words I Love You with events and times that have meaning. By communicating it this way, he'll learn the behavior of saying it back.

LONG WALKS

Taking a long walk together has volumes of lasting benefit for your relationship or marriage no matter what stage you're in or how long you've been together.

Aside from all the romantic reasons, the health aspects alone are reason enough to take long walks, together.

To get this regular event started, put it on your calendar.

It's a good thing to schedule it at a time that both of you can commit to, but it's even better if you mix it up a bit.

For example, take a long walk in a nature preserve on a crisp, cool morning; and, when it's too hot outside, head to a mall or school gym and take the walk inside; and also schedule a walk in the evening and get a double benefit of watching the sunset.

The learned behavior will help you both health wise, keep you fitness minded, and give you plenty of quality time at sunrise, sunset, and should even help boost your communication.

At some point, you, as his woman, will realize that learned behavior has done its job when he is dressed, walking shoes on, and pacing the floor waiting for you when it's time to walk. How's that for a simple, but effective way to teach?

Enjoy!

OPENING DOORS

Chivalry in your Mr. Right is a great quality. But if he's never been taught that he needs to open doors for you, when you're in the car riding together, he'll walk around to his side of the car and leave you to get in the passenger seat on your own. The same is true for when you get to your destination, instead of getting out, walking around and opening the door for you, he'll wait for you get out on your own.

Teaching Chivalry is a challenge if there is no foundation in place to build it on. But, because you're laying it on top of the foundation of learned behavior that you're setting, it's actually quite simple.

So, if he gets in the car before you, stand there until he gets back out, walks around and opens your door. Do the same when he gets out of the car and leaves you sitting there. Sit there until he comes around and opens the door for you to get out. Use the same method when you're on the way into a building, restaurant, church, etc. Stand there until he opens the door for you.

This learned behavior may take force-feeding, but he'll soon start to realize that it's something he's supposed to do naturally. Again, use positive reinforcement by saying, *"Thank You Baby."* Recently, I saw three generations of female members of one family headed toward a door with a young male member of the family. He made it to the door first, opened it, walked in ahead of them, and let the door close behind him. Before I could catch myself I nearly collared him and told him to go back and open the door for those women. The look on his face told me he had no clue why. Sad.

KISSING YOU PASSIONATELY

If you like to kiss, it probably means you like to be kissed. You can help your Mr. Right understand that kissing can be used to enhance foreplay several days before you ever make love.

Passionate kisses, done correctly, can leave a woman breathless, speechless, and in a daze wondering what comes next. Kissing, affects every single part of your body. A passionate kiss involves your lips, the corners of your mouth, every part of the tongue, tickling the roof of your mouth, and even you participating by sticking your tongue in his mouth.

A passionate kiss can be taken to another level, and even be great fun and more sensual if you add a piece of your favorite candy for both of you to share during the kiss.

Every man wants his woman, girlfriend, or wife to be a sex kitten. And, you can go a long way by initiating a kiss, and using your tongue to kiss him. Men love this! It says that you're willing to go a step further in trying to please us.

Kissing doesn't have to always be on the mouth. Kiss the body all over. The sexual energy generated from a passionate kiss can serve as the greatest form of foreplay and can also be a tool for teaching learned behavior.

I could write an entire chapter on this subject, but here are just a few "foreplay-related" examples:

• Go to be earlier than him one night. But before you go to bed, leave him a note on his mirror in the bathroom telling him, *"Baby, you looked really handsome today, I look forward to seeing you in the morning, and I especially look forward to getting one of your truly passionate kisses before you leave for work."*

• Show up, unannounced, at his job on the day you have sex scheduled for that evening. The moment you see him, give him the biggest most passionate kiss you can muster, touch his belt, then leave.

• Get up much earlier than him the morning you have sex scheduled for later that day. Shower, get dressed, and on your way out the door, wake him up with nothing but a trail of kisses all over his face, neck, shoulders and chest, then softly rub his penis and leave.

Be exciting, be creative, be passionate. And remember, the purpose is to teach learned behavior, so he'll start doing these things to you.

HOLDING HANDS

Everywhere we went, no matter where we were, for 29 years I held my wife's hand. Walking, sitting in church, in the car, at functions, even watching TV on the sofa together.

This is a sign that he wants to give you some security, that he's right there, that he's not going anywhere.

Teaching this to your Mr. Right is simple, even if he's not the type to hold hands. And, what I'm about to share with you can be a great tool for teaching this learned behavior.

Here it goes:

If your Mr. Right doesn't automatically reach for your hand, REACH FOR HIS! It's really that simple.

Any and every time you are together, no matter where it is, grab his hand if he doesn't automatically grab yours. This will start to send signals to his brain that this it something you want, what you expect, and that it's a part of togetherness.

Take it a step further and add some sensuality to it every once in a while. How? When you grab his hand, place a simple kiss on the knuckles, or open it and kiss the palm. You can even lick the palm and suck on the fingers as a sign of things to come. He'll enjoy it, and after a while, he'll start associating holding hands with romance and start doing it.

MAKING YOU LAUGH

Making you laugh doesn't mean your Mr. Right has to be or work on suddenly becoming a comedian. While him having a sense of humor certainly helps, for the purpose of training in Learned Behavior, it means you need to teach him how, which ensures that you, get your, regular dose of laughter.

On your calendar, schedule times to visit a comedy club; or just sit and watch a night of your favorite sitcoms. His sense of humor should not only reflect yours, but it should also be compatible, as well as a challenge.

To help your Mr. Right learn to make and keep you laughing, using the same tools we've used thus far, find a local gift shop that sells cards that you know will be amusing to both you and him, and on the day you have a visit to the comedy club or TV night scheduled, leave him a card somewhere saying,

"Hey Honey, I look forward to a night of laughter."
Sign it something to the affect of, *"Your Funny Honey"*.

Be creative. The inspiration for what to say in these cards will come to you, and most importantly, over time, they will start to give him an indication that this is another way to communicate and be ro-mantic. and he'll start doing it without thinking of it, or being told.

And, at some point, he'll start to take the initiative by saying that he also looks forward to sharing such special times of laughter with you, as well.

TOUCHING ANY AND EVERYWHERE

Reading this heading you probably believe that I'm talking about touching on a certain part of your body. And while that is some of what this section is about, I'd also like to focus on how to keep the flame lit and excitement energized in your relationship or marriage by touching each other sensually, sexually, romantically, when you visit certain places as well.

Here are a few examples from my own touching arsenal:

• When we're in church, I hold her hand, or put my arm around her, and every now and then, when we're standing, I rub the nape of her back a little.

• When I'm about to silently stare deep into her eyes, I place the palm of my hand on her cheek. I do the same before kissing her.

• When we're at a place we've gone to sight-see, I'll stand close behind her and wrap my arms over her shoulders. This is a great way to give her the signal that it's time to play 'back that thang up'.

• When we're walking through crowds, I'll stop in the middle of the crowd, turn and face her, grab both her hands, and kiss her. She loves me being spontaneous.

• When we're in the movies, I tickle her knees with my fingers. And if it's dark enough, I'll let my imagination take my wherever it can, without getting us thrown out.

Touching is sensual and reassuring. And in order to teach this to your Mr. Right so it becomes a learned behavior, do the things I just described, to him.

Use these examples, or be creative and generate your own, but use touching as a way to reassure him that you're his.

Here are a few more examples that will get him to learn the behavior of touching:

~ Lightly rub his chest when he's holding you.
~ Secretly rub his penis when you're in a restaurant.
~ Play with the hair on his arms and legs while riding in the car.
~ Stand in front of him and rub your butt against him in an elevator.

Lastly, leave him a note every now and then saying,

"Hi Hotness, I challenge you to find me wherever I am today and secretly touch me in places that no one else notices."

Keeping the flame lit in your relationship and or marriage is not hard, if you are willing to let learned behavior be your guide.

FLIRTING OR IN HIS CASE, BEING Mannish

Teaching a man how to be mannish, may seem difficult to a woman, but it isn't. It's just flirting. And sometimes flirting includes turning up the heat a bit by doing certain things to entice you, but you can teach him how to do these things so it becomes learned behavior.

Here are some flirting techniques I suggest using to help teach him to remember things he did to you when you first met. And the only requirement, is that you do these things when he least expects it, is not looking for it, and doesn't think you would do them.

LIGHT
Whisper in his ear. Squeeze his butt. Nibble on his earlobe.

MEDIUM
Use your tongue to trace the outside of his hips. Place each one of his fingers in your mouth. Lick circles around and under his knees. Put ice cream on his toes and lick it off. Softly kisses on his neck/ shoulders.

HEAVY
Simulate oral sex by rubbing your lips all over the front of his pants. Let him touch you through your panties while on a road trip. Shake your breasts in his face while getting dressed. Let him watch you eat chocolate strawberries. Play with his nipples through his shirt.

Flirting is just a prelude to, and enhancement of foreplay.

Some of these items are things you want him to do to you so you have to be willing to show him what to do, and communicate to him that you want him to do these things to you, in order for him to start doing them as learned behavior.

NUSTLE THE NECK

Your neck has plenty of nerves that can help you teach your Mr. Right to remember what it feels like to be romantic without him thinking that it always leads to sex.

Your neck and shoulders can be Nustled without the need to touch any other part of the body.

It sends a whole range of sensations to other parts of your body, and is one of the most active erogenous zones.

It can be done with just his nose, or just his lips, or just his tongue. Or, it can be done by using a combination of all three.

To give him subtle reminders that you want to feel this sensation from time to time, send him an email or text to his phone one morning while he's at work.

Be forward and up front.

> *"Darling, my neck and shoulders need some attention.*
> *I don't want a massage.*
> *I just want to feel your nose, lips, and tongue on them, for now."*

I don't suggest doing this on the day you have sex scheduled, because it will have the opposite effect of making him associate this action with sex, instead of you teaching this learned behavior as a part of being romantic.

HOT BATHS

Whether you are a woman of the now, or a working mom, or even a Homemaker who stays at home with the kids while he works, every now and then you need some down time to yourself.

On your calendar, at least twice a month, when it's convenient for you, place a time to take in some rest and relaxation, courtesy of your Mr. Right.

Stay in your teaching mode, and give him a mini-itinerary for how you want things to come about such as:

~ *Fill the Tub 1/2 full with Hot Water.*
~ *Add My Favorite Fragrance Bath Oil.*
~ *Make Sure There Are Lots of Bubbles.*
~ *Set a Table Next to the Tub.*
~ *On the Table Place Chocolates, and a Good Book.*
~ *Light a Few Candles For Me.*
              And, most importantly...
~ *Take The Kids and Go Have Fun With Them.*
~ *See You When You Return at _____ [time].*

Again, simple instructions to let him know that you need this from time to time. Afterwards, give him a card saying,

              "Thank you for making my bath time special.
              I look forward to the next one."

And, eventually, he should start preparing this time for you on his own, under the simple effectiveness of learned behavior.

TONGUE ONLY SEX

Sex does not have to always include penetration with his penis. A phenomenal way for your Mr. Right to learn romance without sex is to teach him to please you without 'him' having to be satisfied.

It's a sacrifice for him, that can enhance romance to some of the highest levels. Again, a man's natural instinct is to plant his pole in the hole, at the thought of sex, the talk of sex, the hint of sex.

With this item on the list, you may have to really encourage him and get him to understand that this experience is about pleasing you.

It may be difficult to get him to know that you need to be satisfied without him having to always get some afterwards. So, as you will see on the calendar, I've already placed a couple of days a month whereby you are looking forward to and expecting tongue only sex.

This means that he will lick you, lavish you, eat you, front and back, until you satisfied, without the promise of him getting any. Again, help him 'learn' that this is a sacrifice. It's about you. Not him.

In fact, I suggest that you have him to keep his clothes on so that you, or him, won't be tempted to take this activity to his level.

Remember, your purpose is to teach him that romancing you this way can and most likely will lead to you wanting him so much more by the time you two do come together for your regular sex, you'll be tearing your own panties off.

On the day tongue only sex is scheduled, leave him a voice mail using your most sensuous tone, saying something to the effect that,

"Lover, I've been thinking of and also daydreaming about you
putting your tongue inside me.
I want you to use it to please me in every way.
Bathe me with it all over my body.
Make me know you're the man by eating me
until I can't take anymore.
Then, flip me over and introduce it to my ass.
I look forward." Signed, *"Lover Girl."*

Tongue only sex is an item on the romance list to be used as a way to enhance your regular sex activity by making you want it more.

If your Mr. Right is willing to make the sacrifice, you will teach him the learned behavior that insertion, doesn't always mean intercourse.

Preparation does not always lead to penetration. And oral sex on you does not have to lead to him getting it too.

If you want to mix it up once in a while, eliminate the tongue, and just let him sit across the room, and watch you please yourself.

Enjoy!

PAYING ATTENTION TO YOU

I am a strong believer that communication is key to preventing relationships from breaking down, and marriages from ending in divorce. And this item on the romance list, is one that you will most certainly welcome.

On your calendar, schedule "talk time". Alternate days for you to talk and him to listen, and then for him to talk and you to listen.

Days before your scheduled time, when you have something that you want to discuss, get his opinion about, or just inform him of, without him offering any response on your day, let him know that...

> *"I'm looking forward to talking to you about X.*
> *And, I also look forward to hearing your*
> *thoughts, feelings, and ideas on the subject*
> *after you've had a couple of days to think about it.*
> *Thank you again for taking the time."*

Most importantly, get him to understand that you don't expect him to offer any response on that day. He is just paying attention to you.

After a few times on the calendar, once you've gotten through a few of these days with him just paying attention to you, he will begin to associate how important this learned behavior is to you.

After a while, he will start looking forward to sharing what he wants to talk about, with you on his days too.

CANDLELIGHT DINNERS

Our daily lives are filled with activities that sometimes keep us from taking time to just enjoy what we work so hard for.

Rent and mortgages, utility bills and insurances, car payments and repairs, jobs and social outings, church and fellowship, phones, texts, and emails, are just a small list of things that can take over and begin to stand in the way of you and your Mr. Right taking time to just enjoy a quiet dinner with just the two of you, at home, with silence around you, meaning no TV, or other distractions, and one candle.

Have him cook or prepare the meal. Then, on the next date, you do the same for him. Eventually, he will see this learned behavior for what it is, which is keeping the flame lit between you, literally.

Make the dinner a full one, just like you were ordering at a table in your favorite restaurant: appetizer, salad, main course, drink.

But the reason I say make this dinner "at home", is because there are distractions at the restaurant. Flirty waitresses, handsome waiters, people at other tables, etc. This is time for you to just connect with each other without the noise of others around.

Schedule this time and enjoy it, and it should do wonders for your relationship and or marriage. There's nothing like a quiet dinner for two with a romantic setting, where a candle is the only source of light. And, it's ok to move everything off the table, get up on it, and feed him that sweet spot between your legs as dessert!

WEEKEND GETAWAYS

Different from vacations, romantic weekend getaways can help work wonders in your relationship or marriage to Mr. Right.

Again, the hustle and bustle of daily lives can often get in the way of couples just taking time to relax.

For this item on the romance list, you're going to teach him the learned behavior of looking forward to driving between 1 to 3 hours away from home on a Friday evening when you both get done with work.

Spend the entire weekend enjoying each other's company in places that you probably otherwise would never see, returning Sunday evening.

Call your convention and visitor's association or bureau and ask them to send you a list of every vacation spot in the state.

Then, get a map of the state.

The challenge for you, is to organize dates and places in the form of one hour drives, two hour drives, three hour drives. I do not recommend going more than three hours away for a weekend trip.

On your jaunt, you can see the sights in another city, take in a show, ski, nature hike, visit waterfalls, or just go and relax on the beach somewhere. *Happy Trails!*

LICK MY EARS AND OTHER EROGENOUS ZONES

A woman's ears have been given some kind of special nerve endings that cause tremendous desire and heighten sensuality and drive sexual pleasure through the proverbial roof.

However, there are other erogenous zones that have similar concentration of nerves and also have similar effect, such as the neck, shoulders, corners of the mouth, scalp, feet and toes, the clefts under the arms, behind the knees, the joint where the sides and thighs meet, the thighs, knees, nipples, fingers, etc.

Use these E-zones to teach your Mr. Right learned behavior that can help enhance your pleasure. You need only to communicate with him that these things affect you, tell him how they affect you, and you can have fun just taking time to explore these things without the result being sex.

Remember, romance is the purpose. Learned behavior is the bonus.

Getting him to associate these erogenous zones with romance can be done in a number of ways.

The easiest way, is to schedule a day of exploring; where all you do is set out to discover your erogenous zones and how sensitive they are. Some may be more sensitive to the tongue, tickling, feathers, etc. But the only way you're going to find out so that you can teach him, is to explore then communicate with him, how these things make you feel. Explore and Enjoy!

BODY AND SCALP MASSAGES

Giving you body massages does not mean Mr. Right has to become a masseur, he can also just send you to a day spa. However, in my experience, giving a woman a hot oil body massage after a bath, can be a seriously sensual experience.

Massages help relieve stress, stress causes our muscles to tense up, and tension can prevent orgasms. Let me say that again.

Tension can prevent orgasms.

So, it is vital to take time regularly to be pampered by him or a spa.

I've already placed a couple of days a month on the sample calendar, but I also suggest alternating the days with him giving you the massage one day, and on the other scheduled day, go to the spa.

There will be deep tissue areas that he may not be experienced enough to reach, or massage effectively. These are areas that a trained massage technician can concentrate on.

Again, using subtle ways to communicate, leave him a note to remind him that your spa or massage day is approaching.

"Super Man, just a note to remind you that
I'm sooo looking forward of my upcoming spa day/massage.
And I most certainly look forward to feeling
your masculine hands all over my body."

And, every couple of months, if you surprise him and add in the same treatment for him, by letting him go along with you, he will start looking forward to it even more!

NOTE: If you and your Mr. Right have children, then this is an absolutely essential element in teaching regular massages as learned behavior.

Further, the scalp is truly an erogenous zone that can send you into another level of excitement. On nights that you know you're going to wash your hair, have your Mr. Right massage your scalp either before, or after you wash it.

From my experience, if you even do this just while you're hanging out together in the park, enjoying the sun and all that nature has to offer, it can change the mood from basic to gettin' busy, in no time.

You know what a scalp massage feels like. He probably does not. But when he sees the effect the tips of his fingers have on you, by watching your eyes roll back in your head, and your body start to squirm around under him, hopefully, he'll start to get the message.

/////////// ALSO \\\\\\\\\\

OFF THE SUBJECT A LITTLE, but if you want some peace in your home, especially if you have kids, I also highly recommend giving your kids, from ages 10-18, a spa day every once in a while as well. The lives of kids can be just as stressful and they can use some rest and relaxation just like adults. You'll be surprised at the results!

FOOT RUBS AND TOE SUCKING

A woman's feet are one of the most ignored but most sensual areas on her body.

If you're going to teach your Mr. Right the learned behavior of rubbing your feet, you need to associate it with a stressful event.

That can be as simple as coming home from a hard day's work; or spending a hard day with the kids; or being on your feet for a long walk.

Although it's best to put it on the calendar, there may be times when you have stressful days that aren't associated with any planned events on your calendar.

So, when you're out and about, either at work, or just hanging out at the mall, or even at home with the kids, but you end up having a stressful day, send your Mr. Right a text, or email, or call him, or leave a voice mail and communicate it to him.

Tell him that you need him to do exactly what you want done.

"Baby, I'm having a hard day on my feet.
I would really appreciate if you could rub my feet later."

Hear me when I say this: most women never ever rub the feet of their Mr. Right, but if you start doing it to him, he may feel the need to reciprocate. Other than oral sex, men rarely like to see you doing something to him he hasn't done to you.

Let me remind you that your Mr. Right may not want to rub or even touch your feet if they look like you've been running through a field of land minds with no shoes on. That means they look 'jacked-up', with corns, calluses, dead skin, bunions, dry, ashy, and on and on.

No water + No oil = NO Foot Rub
and definitely no toe sucking!

Take time to visit the salon every once in a while
and let them give you a nice pedicure.

Another extremely sensual way of getting you in a romantic mood for the same day, or even later that week, or even during sex, is for your Mr. Right to spend some time licking your feet and sucking on your toes.

If you want your Mr. Right to take it a step further, and learn the behavior because he associates it with you getting extremely horny, let him drip and eat ice cream off your toes. Feet are erogenous zones, they are ticklish, and that often makes them very sensitive and highly sensual.

If done correctly, teaching this learned behavior can bring you great pleasure. But again, get a pedicure. I recommend placing it on your calendar as a regularly monthly event, so that when the time or the moment comes, you don't need to be worried that your feet are full of corns, calluses, dead skin, and bunions, that serve as a huge turn off to just about any man. So, pedicure, pedicure, pedicure. Enjoy!

COMMUNICATING AND LISTENING

Here are some known facts in the areas of communicating between men and women:

Men think women talk too much.
Women think men don't talk enough.

Men think women talk about stuff he doesn't want to hear.
Women think men don't listen at what they have to say.

Men and women place different types of values on things.

This is the primary reason for lack of communication between men and women.

Men are physical.
Women are emotional.

Women place their emotions first.
Men place their emotions last.

Women place physics last.
Men place physics first.

Women love to talk.
Men hate to listen.

Finding common ground, through learned behavior helps.

The value a man places on you and your relationship or marriage determines the level of communication and amount of listening you should expect to receive in any normal relationship or marriage.

However, there is a way to teach communication to your Mr. Right, as learned behavior.

Here's how: using your calendar, place a date on the schedule where the two of you will do nothing except sit down, without distractions, and talk. One day you talk and he can listen and take notes. The other day he will talk and you can listen and take notes.

This will help start and keep lines of communication open about any and every subject. And, you should start using other ways to communicate "with romance in mind" such as email, text, cards, love letters, poetry, etc.

Take time to talk to each other. Then make a separate time to just listen to each other. You can't listen well while you're talking. So when it's your day to talk, have him to just listen. Then give him the same courtesy when it's his day to talk, you just listen.

Lack of communication is in the top 3 reasons people divorce
Lack of communication is in the top three reasons that relationships break down and marriages end in divorce. Therefore, this item on the romance list is easily and by far, one of the most important.

The most popular way between my wife and I, is praying together.

FLOWERS, CARDS, GIFTS, CANDY, POETRY

Post-Sex, as part of romance, for no reason at all, or just because your Mr. Right appreciates you, you should receive regular things such as flowers, cards, gifts, candy, and poetry.

In order to teach this as a learned behavior, you need to start the process by giving these things to him first. when's the last time you took flowers to him, on his job? At his school?

Men hate when women outdo them, in any area of a relationship and often time in many areas of life, so if you start showering him with these things, he will feel the need to do the same.

On your sample romance calendar, I've already placed a couple of dates as reminders for him to bring, not send, flowers to your job.

The reason he needs to 'bring' them is because if he just picks up the phone and just has them sent to you, he'll likely forget it when the time comes to do it again. So, having him physically drive to the store, pick them out, have them wrapped, take them to the car, driving to your job, then delivering them, will keep the actual event in his mind for quite some time.

Most people forget even phone calls we made just yesterday without looking in our phone first. But, the action of going to the store, buying the flowers, driving to your location, and bringing them to you, not only helps him remember, it will earn him brownie points with you, and with your co-workers.

When he starts associating this learned behavior with getting some positive feedback and accolades from the people who see the flowers, he will start to remember and remind himself to do it more often. The same concept is true for cards, candy and gifts.

And, on your calendar, I've mixed it up a bit by alternating the delivery of flowers one week, and candy the next.

Again, showering him with these things on a regular basis if he isn't used to doing these things for you, will trigger a natural male instinct within him, not to be outdone by a woman.

So, it will have an effect on him, and incite him to respond. That response is the learned behavior you're looking for.

In terms of writing poetry to each other, I suggest making this twice a month as well. Be creative, but most importantly, be consistent.

Use your phone as a way to surprise him with poetry every now and then. Send him a poem via text. Find the words. If you don't know where to start, don't worry, reach back to the old-faithfuls of 'Roses are red, violets are blue, etc.'

Eventually, you'll start to let the poetic words flow by using every situation, thought, fantasy, etc., as a springboard to great poems.

Enjoy!

SILENTLY STARE DEEP INTO MY EYES

One of the lost arts of being romantic is staring deeply into someone's eyes without saying a word.

Silence itself, is a form of romantic communication, and if done with the intent that it is purposed, can be extremely sensual, thought provoking and profound.

Many people say that the eyes are the window to the soul. Because of this belief, I'm challenging you to try and discover just what is behind your Mr. Right's eyes, by asking him to stare into yours.

This learned behavior can reveal many truths when you are happy, sad, lonely, hurting, or just needing to be held.

Many people wear their emotions on their faces, and the eyes are the outlets for those.

You can't see sadness, hurt, pain, happiness, joy, or even a smile, until and unless you look into someone's face.

So make it a practice to just take time to remove all distractions, sit down, and communicate with each other in silence.

Silence is golden. Proving it, is platinum!

Whatever you do, resist the urge to break the silence by talking. Just be still. Be silent. Let your hearts talk to each other. You'll see why.

SPOON WITH ME

Women are often constantly complaining that men don't want to hold them until they fall asleep.

You can teach your Mr. Right to learn this behavior by simply forcing it upon him enough times that he starts to get the message.

When you're in bed together, don't let him turn over and go to sleep leaving you to do the same. Turn your back to him, slide over to his side, and force him to share his body and body heat with you, or force him right out the other side of the bed. He will begin to either turn and face your back, thereby causing his body to spoon with yours, or he will try to find some way out of it. Don't let it happen.

This is another one of those learned behaviors that may need to be force-fed on him, but what you need to help him to understand is that you need it, want it, and so should he.

It's a very good way to show affection to you and from you to him, and it's the sign that you are connected in the most intimate of ways.

Most men, will try and give you the excuse that when he spoons you, his penis is rubbing against your butt, thereby causing a hard on, and if you don't plan to use it, he doesn't want to go through the agony of falling to sleep thinking about it. Tell him these words, "B.S.", because he's already thinking about it before bed, in bed, and while sleep, so tell him to deal with it, or go sleep somewhere else. Period.

DANCE LESSONS, SKATING, AND SHOWS

Some of the most popular shows on television today involve dancing. And, it's one of the most romantic ways for couples to keep the fire lit in relationships and marriages.

There are plenty of places to take dance lessons of every type, and my only recommendation it to find one that works for the both of you, and enjoy it.

Don't place a hurdle in front of yourself by focusing on the type of dance. If you like Samba and he doesn't, because he doesn't want to move his hips or has no rhythm, tell him he can "learn" and that the purpose his is not to master the dance, just to have fun doing it.

If he puts up an argument, don't fight it, just ask him to pick a type of dance that he likes, and go with him. Then, once that class is over, and you've done what he wanted, remind him of it, grab his hand, and take him right back to the Samba class.

Going to see a ballroom dancing competition is a great way to have fun, and see the amazing talent out there, but I would be careful not to take your Mr. Right to any place where the women are half dressed.

Remember, he's still a man.

Slow dancing to melodic music such as jazz, R N B, smooth big band tunes, and even some slow pop songs, is a tremendous way to connect with each other and be romantic.

Light some candles, remove all distractions, and give each other the time you deserve.

Teaching the learned behavior of wanting to dance is not difficult, if you can get him past the first hurdle of not wanting to do it.

So, schedule it, take him with you, and get out on the floor.

Skating, whether it be ice skating, roller-blading, or roller skating, has tremendous benefits for your health and is truly romantic. Many movies have shown romantic scenes of couples ice skating in a park during the Christmas season. But just going to roller skate together is fun. If you don't know how, ask someone at the rink to help you. And, buying rollerblades is a great way to get out and get some needed exercise, enjoy nature, and spend time together.

Teaching dancing and skating as a learned behavior can be quite challenging, but once the activity is started, both of you will get great benefits from it.

Shows are no different. There are dozens upon dozens of great shows in theatres in your town or nearby right now. And there always are. Take advantage of this and get out of the house and go enjoy them.

There are so many opportunities to take in a show, play, etc., or even finding and following flash mobs around can be fun.

Get to it and enjoy!

TAKE CLASSES TOGETHER

Back in the Compatibility chapter, I discussed how great it is for couples to be compatible intellectually, educationally, etc. However, to teach this learned behavior you don't even have to be compatible in this area, just have similar interests in wanting to learn something new.

For example, there are numerous Community Education Programs that have free classes, as well as extremely low cost ones that can help you learn everything from computers to candle-making, glass blowing to gardening.

And, it's a great way to spend time together.

These are special times that couples need to embrace in order to help keep the flame lit between them.

Schedule something every other month. Then do as much research on it as you can, sit down with him and discuss it, then take the class.

Whether it's an activity that only takes a night, week, or month to learn, you're spending time with each other.

And if you want to take it a step further, enroll in a longer class with the purpose of a certificate or degree in mind, and you'll get even more benefit.

Whatever it is, just do it.

NOW YOU HAVE IT

Now that you've been given a whole list of things to do, to help start, keep and rekindle the romantic flame that was lit between the two of you during the Pre-Sex stage, there should be no excuse for you not to start and keep enjoying your relationship and marriage with your Mr. Right.

Learned Behavior is not a new strategy. It is a proven concept that when put to good use, has some fantastic benefits for couples who take the time to put in the work necessary to make your relationship and marriage work.

Yes, it takes work.

But if it's worth it to you to try and hold on to your Mr. Right, then it's more than worth it to work toward it.

You worked hard to get it, or he worked hard to get you, so keep it. What started out as romance, can most certainly continue to be just that, romantic. Be creative, mix it up, whatever it takes, but just be consistent, and committed.

Attention: Sex-Ed teachers: Although my comment about female sex-ed teachers being responsible for many relationships that break down and marriages that end in divorce, may be harsh, I still believe the *art of romance* should be taught before the *act of reproduction*, and there's really not much more I can add to that subject.

AND...

Sometimes you need to separate to appreciate. Don't separate a long time. But take a few days in order to appreciate each other by missing one another. It helps.

If you look on the Romance Calendar, you'll notice that I placed days where you only call each other, but not see each other.

There's an old saying that familiarity breeds contempt, but the truth is, it doesn't have to.

There's another old saying that absence makes the heart grow fonder.

But, whichever of these adages you subscribe to, remember, romance in any relationship can be a wonderful, continuous, exciting, journey between two people that helps keep the foreplay and the fire lit.

CHAPTER SEVEN

COMMUNICATE

COMMUNICATION
Listening, Writing, Texting, Talking

Unlike in the mid-80's when my wife and I got together, today, there are all kinds of ways for couples to communicate. And, regardless of how you do it, just get it done.

Communication is one of the most important keys to building, and keeping your relationship with Mr. Right. It helps keep you focused, aligned, interested, and a host of other things, as long as the communication between you two, is open and honest.

Women often say that your man can talk to you about anything. But you rarely mean that. Why? Because some of the conversations my wife and I had in the past, could ruin our relationship today. So I've adjusted accordingly, and only share with her what I need her opinion, input, prayer, or follow up on.

Be careful how you approach sensitive subjects, but find common ground that leads to open, honest, and regular communication. Words can hurt. So be careful what you say to each other. The wrong words can lead to roads you don't need to travel, and also open up doors from the past that unleash previous damage, destruction, pain, anger, and all kinds of other emotional scars. The kind that can tear relationships apart. For the sake of conversation, you have to be willing and able to communicate, but know that you have to also be tactful doing it.

Writing can be a tremendous way to share you feelings with your Mr. Right, if you aren't the talkative type. The same is true for him.

My wife and I have written dozens of letters to each other in every situation. Sometimes writing letters can help you say what won't come out of your mouth or heart.

It doesn't matter what form of communication you use, as long as you communicate.

Remember, listening is just as important as talking. You both can't talk at the same time, otherwise, someone is not listening.

Enjoy any and every time you take on your Romance Calendar to set aside time to communicate. It will do wonders for your marriage, and your relationship to Mr. Right.

Most men are not natural communicators, when it comes to women. Sure, we can spit game, bring a strong rap, and even come up with the most creative lines on the planet when we're trying to get into your panties, but Post-sex, many men get tongue tied, leaving women to complain about him not talking to you.

Teaching communication as a learned behavior to your Mr. Right is a necessity, so use whatever form you can to start it, and to keep it.

Reminder: Men who don't talk much, are great listeners. But if you want your Mr. Right to do more than that, you have to teach him.

The Romance Calendar is a way of communicating. If you want your Mr. Right to do certain things at specific times how else will he know if you don't communicate that?

~ Tell him

~ Teach him

~ Train him

~ Show him

...use whatever method you need to, but communicate it to him.

MEN ARE NOT MIND READERS

AND

MOST OF THE TIME OUR MINDS ARE ON SEX ANYWAY

Knowing this, unless you have openly communicated what you need, want, expect, how you want it done, and when, and also under what conditions there can be an alteration to your plan, you should not be expecting him to do what you have not communicated to him to do.

Women often say, it's his responsibility to already know!

But I've written the material in the pages of this book to help you fully become aware and hopefully understand, that is rarely the case.

Remember

Men are conquerors. Women are courters.

And, our individual need for communication is based on those two very different characteristics.

CONQUERORS...

Communicate very little. By nature, we keep our plans secret until we find it necessary to reveal them, which leads to women saying we don't talk enough. And, we only discuss what we place value on. Anything else, to us, is irrelevant.

COURTERS...

Communicate quite often. Because of the very nature of courting, women expect open and honest and constant communication about their relationships or any topic of the day, which leads to men saying women talk too much. To you, everything is relevant.

Therefore, find ways, learn ways, take classes on ways, to start, keep, and relight the fires of communication between you.

Because couples that don't communicate, don't court.

**And if there's no courting,
it often leads to less conquering.**

**And if there's less conquering,
men will often search for another conquest.**

BASIC RELATIONSHIP QUESTIONS
TO ASK YOURSELF

- Choice: *can you live with this as a choice?*
- Character: *can you accept this is part of his character?*
- Compromise: *is this a trait you can compromise on?*
- Conform: *Can you help him conform this behavior?*
- Compatibility: *Do you have the same or similar trait?*
- Challenge: *Can you teach this trait as learned behavior?*

CHAPTER EIGHT

CREATING YOUR MR. RIGHT WISH LIST

CREATING YOUR MR. RIGHT WISH LIST

As I eluded to in the Introduction, finding your Mr. Right, or him finding you, if often like gambling against the odds like public lotteries. Most men, are Mr. Everything during the Pre-Sex Stage because we're wired to do any and everything you want us to, just right, in order for you to believe that we are perfect for you. However, in the vast majority of men, keeping up or even remembering the level of romance and activity you experienced from us pre-sex, is nearly impossible to maintain post-sex.

Once you've had sex with your Mr. Right, the conquer is over for him. The conquest, won. He tends to relax from romance, and focus more on repeating the act of reproduction, sticking his pole in the hole, and most women will recognize a change almost immediately.

Again, the things he did before you had sex with him, aren't as vital to him after sex. It's not intentional. It's how he's wired as a teen. He actually knows better, but he doesn't know the lasting effects that you having sex with him has just had on the part of his being that associates romance with something he places value on.

Before you had sex, being romantic had a stratospheric value to him, because it was the tool he needed to use to woo you into bed. Once sex took place, he feels that tool is no longer needed. And, the more sex you give him without requiring him to be romantic, the less value he places on romance. Therefore, over time, he starts to ignore it, and even forget parts of what it takes to even be romantic.

In this book, **_Romance 101_**, the Course material is a compilation of research, reality, and recollection.

For the list, I used three criteria for coming up with 100 names and definitions that if studied and applied, can help create your own wish list, for your Mr. Right.

REMINDER:

>your *Choices*,
>
>the *Characteristics* you look for,
>
>any *Compromises* you are willing to make,
>
>helping to *Conform* his past behavior,
>
>and learning about your areas of *Compatibility*,

all lead up to a simple *Challenge* to teach your Mr. Right, using the concept of learned behavior and proven strategies, how to be and stay romantic, and enable you to measure his progress using the *Charts* I've outlined in this book.

Here's the list. No man will have them all, but should at least have a good combination of some.

THE MR. RIGHT WISH LIST

Before we get into the list, I mentioned very early in the book that you have six things to focus on when creating this list:

1. Can you live with the choices you make?
2. Can you accept certain things as part of his character?
3. Are you willing to compromise on certain traits he has?
4. Are you ready to help him conform some bahaviors?
5. Are you compatible in certain areas?
6. Are you willing to teach him learned behavior?

A LETTER TO MYSELF

My Name is [your name goes here], and I'm looking for Mr. Right. I want him to be [culture goes here], he must also be [height goes here], with an [type of body goes here, average, hard or workable for example]. And, he must like [your adjectives for non-compromise goes here], with the ability to [buy me nice things for example] , as well as [take care of me financially for example]. Above all, he should [like my mother, parents, family for example], as well as be [rooted and grounded in his career for example]. I'll stop there. You finish.

Just like you've been instructed on the various things to do to teach Mr. Right learned behavior. Here's something just for you. Once you're done filling in the blanks in this letter to yourself, post it where you can see it, and only take it down once it is fulfilled.

ABJECT : Hopeless, Miserable, Dismal.

MY ADVICE: You don't want this on your Mr. Right Wish List.
Why? Because if you're lively and outgoing, his comfort zone is
going to be the exact opposite of where yours is.

• Choice: *can you live with this as a choice?*
• Character: *can you accept this is part of his character?*
• Compromise: *is this a trait you can compromise on?*
• Conform: *Can you help him conform this behavior?*
• Compatibility: *Do you have the same or similar trait?*
• Challenge: *Can you teach this trait as learned behavior?*

Reminder: The purpose is to create your Mr. Right Wish List.

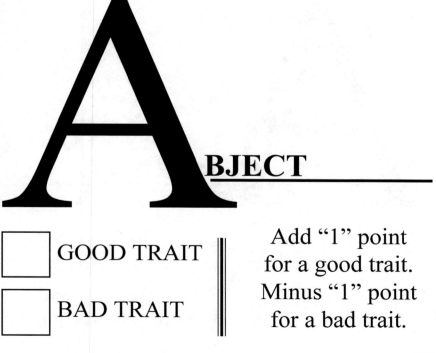

ABJECT

GOOD TRAIT

BAD TRAIT

Add "1" point
for a good trait.
Minus "1" point
for a bad trait.

ABSOLUTE : Grounded, knowledgeable.

MY ADVICE: You want this on your Mr. Right Wish List.
Why? Because he makes decisions based on solid research, rather than what society says, the slant of the media, or wishful thinking.

- Choice: *can you live with this as a choice?*
- Character: *can you accept this is part of his character?*
- Compromise: *is this a trait you can compromise on?*
- Conform: *Can you help him conform this behavior?*
- Compatibility: *Do you have the same or similar trait?*
- Challenge: *Can you teach this trait as learned behavior?*

Reminder: The purpose is to create your Mr. Right Wish List.

☐ GOOD TRAIT

☐ BAD TRAIT

Add "1" point
for a good trait.
Minus "1" point
for a bad trait.

ATTENTIVE : Thoughtful, considerate, dutiful.

MY ADVICE: You want this on your Mr. Right Wish List.
Why? Because he pays special attention to your needs and considers
it his duty to please you.

- Choice: *can you live with this as a choice?*
- Character: *can you accept this is part of his character?*
- Compromise: *is this a trait you can compromise on?*
- Conform: *Can you help him conform this behavior?*
- Compatibility: *Do you have the same or similar trait?*
- Challenge: *Can you teach this trait as learned behavior?*

> **Reminder: The purpose is to create your Mr. Right Wish List.**

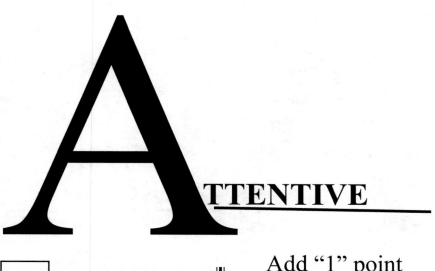

GOOD TRAIT

BAD TRAIT

Add "1" point
for a good trait.
Minus "1" point
for a bad trait.

ATTRACTIVE: Good-looking. Appealing. Eye-catching.

MY ADVICE: You want this on your Mr. Right Wish List.
Why? Because if you're not attractive to him, inside and out, it's quite likely that the two of you won't be together long.

- Choice: *can you live with this as a choice?*
- Character: *can you accept this is part of his character?*
- Compromise: *is this a trait you can compromise on?*
- Conform: *Can you help him conform this behavior?*
- Compatibility: *Do you have the same or similar trait?*
- Challenge: *Can you teach this trait as learned behavior?*

Reminder: The purpose is to create your Mr. Right Wish List.

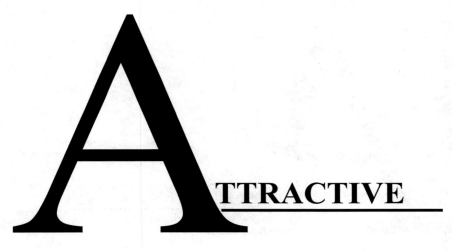

□ GOOD TRAIT

□ BAD TRAIT

Add "1" point for a good trait. Minus "1" point for a bad trait.

AFFECTIONATE : Loving. Warm. Friendly. Kind.

MY ADVICE: You want this on your Mr. Right Wish List.
Why? Because he's naturally attentive; he most likely understands
chivalry: opens doors, pulls out chairs, holds hands, kisses, etc.

- Choice: *can you live with this as a choice?*
- Character: *can you accept this is part of his character?*
- Compromise: *is this a trait you can compromise on?*
- Conform: *Can you help him conform this behavior?*
- Compatibility: *Do you have the same or similar trait?*
- Challenge: *Can you teach this trait as learned behavior?*

Reminder: The purpose is to create your Mr. Right Wish List.

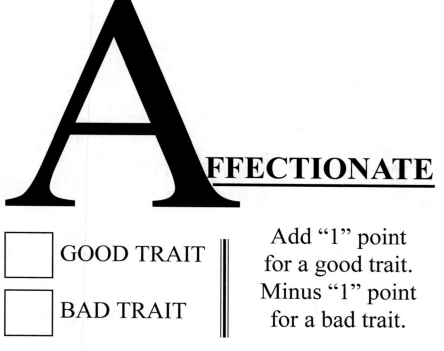

AFFECTIONATE

☐ GOOD TRAIT

☐ BAD TRAIT

Add "1" point for a good trait.
Minus "1" point for a bad trait.

ADJUSTABLE : Adaptable. Flexible. Amenable.

MY ADVICE: You want this on your Mr. Right Wish List.
Why? Because he's the type that recognizes when something isn't going right one way, is open to trying it a new way on another day.

- Choice: *can you live with this as a choice?*
- Character: *can you accept this is part of his character?*
- Compromise: *is this a trait you can compromise on?*
- Conform: *Can you help him conform this behavior?*
- Compatibility: *Do you have the same or similar trait?*
- Challenge: *Can you teach this trait as learned behavior?*

Reminder: The purpose is to create your Mr. Right Wish List.

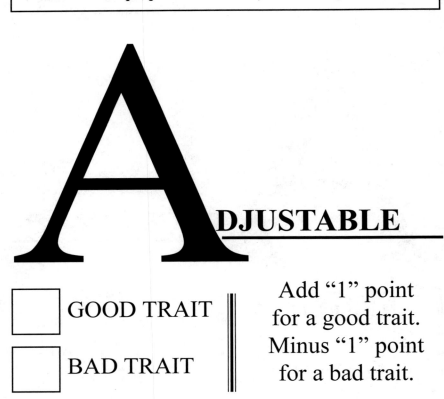

GOOD TRAIT

BAD TRAIT

Add "1" point for a good trait. Minus "1" point for a bad trait.

ABSOLVING : Forgiving. Releasing. Freeing.

MY ADVICE: You want this on your Mr. Right Wish List.
Why? Because he's the type not to hold on to things in order to bring them up in an argument later.

- Choice: *can you live with this as a choice?*
- Character: *can you accept this is part of his character?*
- Compromise: *is this a trait you can compromise on?*
- Conform: *Can you help him conform this behavior?*
- Compatibility: *Do you have the same or similar trait?*
- Challenge: *Can you teach this trait as learned behavior?*

> **Reminder: The purpose is to create your Mr. Right Wish List.**

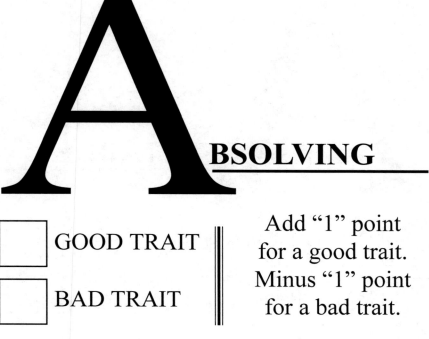

ABSOLVING

GOOD TRAIT

BAD TRAIT

Add "1" point for a good trait.
Minus "1" point for a bad trait.

ADAPTABLE : Workable. Modifiable.

MY ADVICE: You want this on your Mr. Right Wish List.
Why? Because he's the type that if his way doesn't work, is willing
to listen to your way, or even a suggested alternate route.

- Choice: *can you live with this as a choice?*
- Character: *can you accept this is part of his character?*
- Compromise: *is this a trait you can compromise on?*
- Conform: *Can you help him conform this behavior?*
- Compatibility: *Do you have the same or similar trait?*
- Challenge: *Can you teach this trait as learned behavior?*

Reminder: The purpose is to create your Mr. Right Wish List.

☐ GOOD TRAIT

☐ BAD TRAIT

Add "1" point
for a good trait.
Minus "1" point
for a bad trait.

ALPHA : Breadwinner. Husband. Father. Leader. Protector.

MY ADVICE: You want this on your Mr. Right Wish List.
Why? Because he gets up early and meets the day head on, and does
the same in other areas of his life, including problems.

- Choice: *can you live with this as a choice?*
- Character: *can you accept this is part of his character?*
- Compromise: *is this a trait you can compromise on?*
- Conform: *Can you help him conform this behavior?*
- Compatibility: *Do you have the same or similar trait?*
- Challenge: *Can you teach this trait as learned behavior?*

Reminder: The purpose is to create your Mr. Right Wish List.

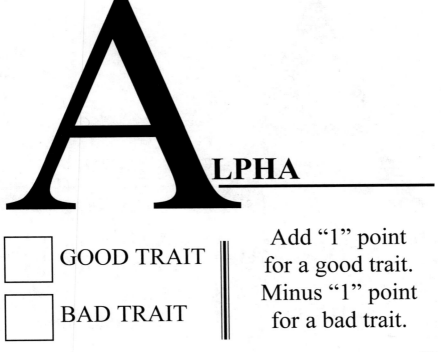

GOOD TRAIT

BAD TRAIT

Add "1" point
for a good trait.
Minus "1" point
for a bad trait.

ASSOCIATED : Linked. Connected. Allied.

MY ADVICE: You want this on your Mr. Right Wish List.
Why? Because he surrounds himself with the right people in order
to help ensure success in various areas.

- Choice: *can you live with this as a choice?*
- Character: *can you accept this is part of his character?*
- Compromise: *is this a trait you can compromise on?*
- Conform: *Can you help him conform this behavior?*
- Compatibility: *Do you have the same or similar trait?*
- Challenge: *Can you teach this trait as learned behavior?*

Reminder: The purpose is to create your Mr. Right Wish List.

☐ GOOD TRAIT

☐ BAD TRAIT

Add "1" point
for a good trait.
Minus "1" point
for a bad trait.

ANGELIC : Knows Church. Understands Ministry.

MY ADVICE: You want this on your Mr. Right Wish List.
Why? Because he believes in God, has a relationship with Him, and
practices his faith by putting it into action.

- Choice: *can you live with this as a choice?*
- Character: *can you accept this is part of his character?*
- Compromise: *is this a trait you can compromise on?*
- Conform: *Can you help him conform this behavior?*
- Compatibility: *Do you have the same or similar trait?*
- Challenge: *Can you teach this trait as learned behavior?*

Reminder: The purpose is to create your Mr. Right Wish List.

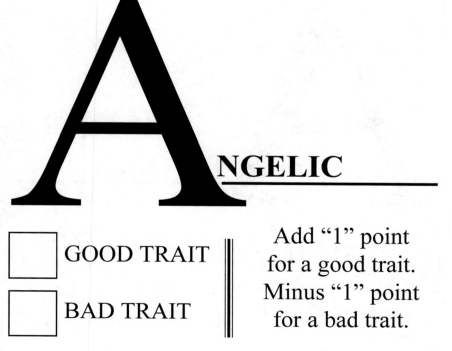

ANGELIC

☐ GOOD TRAIT

☐ BAD TRAIT

Add "1" point
for a good trait.
Minus "1" point
for a bad trait.

ANATOMICAL : Real Man.

MY ADVICE: You want this on your Mr. Right Wish List.
Why? Because he is without surgical enhancements, steroids, or other modifications to try and be more of a man than he actually is.

- Choice: *can you live with this as a choice?*
- Character: *can you accept this is part of his character?*
- Compromise: *is this a trait you can compromise on?*
- Conform: *Can you help him conform this behavior?*
- Compatibility: *Do you have the same or similar trait?*
- Challenge: *Can you teach this trait as learned behavior?*

Reminder: The purpose is to create your Mr. Right Wish List.

ANATOMICAL

☐ GOOD TRAIT

☐ BAD TRAIT

Add "1" point for a good trait. Minus "1" point for a bad trait.

ACCOMPLISHED : Cultured. Learned. Cultivated.

MY ADVICE: You want this on your Mr. Right Wish List.
Why? Because he is the type to take you to plays, opera, concerts, the symphony, dancing, and isn't embarrassed if his friends know it.

- Choice: *can you live with this as a choice?*
- Character: *can you accept this is part of his character?*
- Compromise: *is this a trait you can compromise on?*
- Conform: *Can you help him conform this behavior?*
- Compatibility: *Do you have the same or similar trait?*
- Challenge: *Can you teach this trait as learned behavior?*

Reminder: The purpose is to create your Mr. Right Wish List.

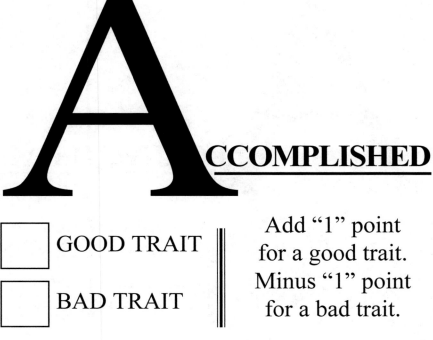

GOOD TRAIT

BAD TRAIT

Add "1" point
for a good trait.
Minus "1" point
for a bad trait.

ARCHITECTURAL : Multidimensional.

MY ADVICE: You want this on your Mr. Right Wish List.
Why? Because he's the type to fix something if it breaks, or builds something if it's needed. Doesn't live alone in his own tunnel vision.

- Choice: *can you live with this as a choice?*
- Character: *can you accept this is part of his character?*
- Compromise: *is this a trait you can compromise on?*
- Conform: *Can you help him conform this behavior?*
- Compatibility: *Do you have the same or similar trait?*
- Challenge: *Can you teach this trait as learned behavior?*

Reminder: The purpose is to create your Mr. Right Wish List.

A RCHITECTURAL

☐ GOOD TRAIT

☐ BAD TRAIT

Add "1" point for a good trait. Minus "1" point for a bad trait.

AVERAGE : Regular. Common. Typical.

MY ADVICE: You want this on your Mr. Right Wish List.
Why? Because if this is what you want, voila! He's at the zero mark.
Any improvements make him above-average.

- Choice: *can you live with this as a choice?*
- Character: *can you accept this is part of his character?*
- Compromise: *is this a trait you can compromise on?*
- Conform: *Can you help him conform this behavior?*
- Compatibility: *Do you have the same or similar trait?*
- Challenge: *Can you teach this trait as learned behavior?*

> **Reminder: The purpose is to create your Mr. Right Wish List.**

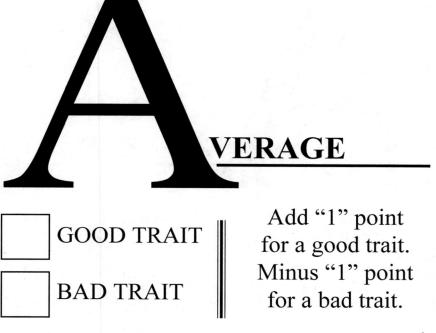

AVERAGE

☐ GOOD TRAIT

☐ BAD TRAIT

Add "1" point
for a good trait.
Minus "1" point
for a bad trait.

ANOINTED : Divinely led.

MY ADVICE: You want this on your Mr. Right Wish List.
Why? Because he is the type that opens his mouth and people listen.
And is a leader without explanation and what he teaches, others learn.

- Choice: *can you live with this as a choice?*
- Character: *can you accept this is part of his character?*
- Compromise: *is this a trait you can compromise on?*
- Conform: *Can you help him conform this behavior?*
- Compatibility: *Do you have the same or similar trait?*
- Challenge: *Can you teach this trait as learned behavior?*

Reminder: The purpose is to create your Mr. Right Wish List.

NOINTED

☐ GOOD TRAIT

☐ BAD TRAIT

Add "1" point
for a good trait.
Minus "1" point
for a bad trait.

ACCEPTING : Tolerant. Patient.

MY ADVICE: You want this on your Mr. Right Wish List.
Why? Because he is type who can wait on things he doesn't like in you, to get better, without criticism. Believes in the best in people.

- Choice: *can you live with this as a choice?*
- Character: *can you accept this is part of his character?*
- Compromise: *is this a trait you can compromise on?*
- Conform: *Can you help him conform this behavior?*
- Compatibility: *Do you have the same or similar trait?*
- Challenge: *Can you teach this trait as learned behavior?*

Reminder: The purpose is to create your Mr. Right Wish List.

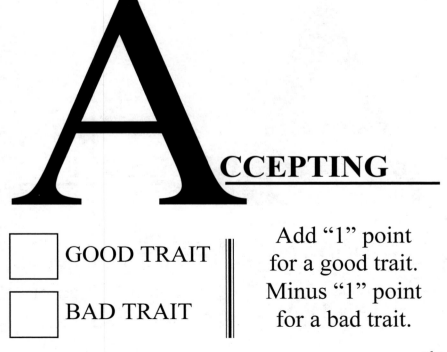

| | GOOD TRAIL | Add "1" point for a good trait. |
| | BAD TRAIT | Minus "1" point for a bad trait. |

AGREEABLE : Pleasant. Enjoyable.

MY ADVICE: You want this on your Mr. Right Wish List.
Why? Because he is not the type who always has to have the final say, or the last word.

- Choice: *can you live with this as a choice?*
- Character: *can you accept this is part of his character?*
- Compromise: *is this a trait you can compromise on?*
- Conform: *Can you help him conform this behavior?*
- Compatibility: *Do you have the same or similar trait?*
- Challenge: *Can you teach this trait as learned behavior?*

Reminder: The purpose is to create your Mr. Right Wish List.

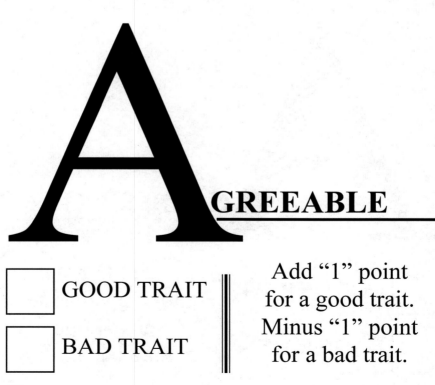

GREEABLE

☐ GOOD TRAIT

☐ BAD TRAIT

Add "1" point for a good trait. Minus "1" point for a bad trait.

ACKNOWLEDGING : Admitting. Conceding.

MY ADVICE: You want this on your Mr. Right Wish List.
Why? Because he is the type who notices things you do and goes out of his way to compliment you for them.

- Choice: *can you live with this as a choice?*
- Character: *can you accept this is part of his character?*
- Compromise: *is this a trait you can compromise on?*
- Conform: *Can you help him conform this behavior?*
- Compatibility: *Do you have the same or similar trait?*
- Challenge: *Can you teach this trait as learned behavior?*

Reminder: The purpose is to create your Mr. Right Wish List.

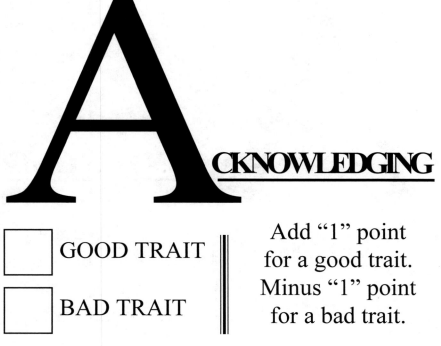

☐ GOOD TRAIT

☐ BAD TRAIT

Add "1" point for a good trait.
Minus "1" point for a bad trait.

ACCENTUATING : Emphasizing. Highlighting.

MY ADVICE: You want this on your Mr. Right Wish List.
Why? Because he is the type that enhances what you already have;
your environment, family, goals, dreams, etc, just by being with you.

- Choice: *can you live with this as a choice?*
- Character: *can you accept this is part of his character?*
- Compromise: *is this a trait you can compromise on?*
- Conform: *Can you help him conform this behavior?*
- Compatibility: *Do you have the same or similar trait?*
- Challenge: *Can you teach this trait as learned behavior?*

Reminder: The purpose is to create your Mr. Right Wish List.

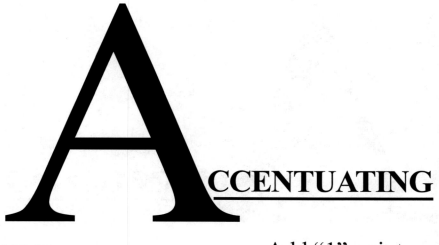

☐ GOOD TRAIT

☐ BAD TRAIT

Add "1" point
for a good trait.
Minus "1" point
for a bad trait.

ACTING : Dramatic. Overly emotional.

MY ADVICE: You "do not" want this on your Mr. Right Wish List. Why? Because he's the type that most women would call a drama queen, and most heterosexual men would call gay. Doesn't know his own truth.

- Choice: *can you live with this as a choice?*
- Character: *can you accept this is part of his character?*
- Compromise: *is this a trait you can compromise on?*
- Conform: *Can you help him conform this behavior?*
- Compatibility: *Do you have the same or similar trait?*
- Challenge: *Can you teach this trait as learned behavior?*

> **Reminder: The purpose is to create your Mr. Right Wish List.**

CTING

| GOOD TRAIT | Add "1" point for a good trait. |
| BAD TRAIT | Minus "1" point for a bad trait. |

ASCENDING : Rising. Climbing. Reaching.

MY ADVICE: You want this on your Mr. Right Wish List.
Why? Because he isn't the type to just stand still, but is striving to
make progress in most or all areas of his life. Never gives up.

- Choice: *can you live with this as a choice?*
- Character: *can you accept this is part of his character?*
- Compromise: *is this a trait you can compromise on?*
- Conform: *Can you help him conform this behavior?*
- Compatibility: *Do you have the same or similar trait?*
- Challenge: *Can you teach this trait as learned behavior?*

> **Reminder: The purpose is to create your Mr. Right Wish List.**

☐ GOOD TRAIT

☐ BAD TRAIT

Add "1" point
for a good trait.
Minus "1" point
for a bad trait.

ATHLETIC: Sporty. Muscular.

MY ADVICE: You want this on your Mr. Right Wish List.
Why? Because he hates couch potatoes. He is fitness minded. Health conscious. And if you aren't, can help you get there without judging.

- Choice: *can you live with this as a choice?*
- Character: *can you accept this is part of his character?*
- Compromise: *is this a trait you can compromise on?*
- Conform: *Can you help him conform this behavior?*
- Compatibility: *Do you have the same or similar trait?*
- Challenge: *Can you teach this trait as learned behavior?*

Reminder: The purpose is to create your Mr. Right Wish List.

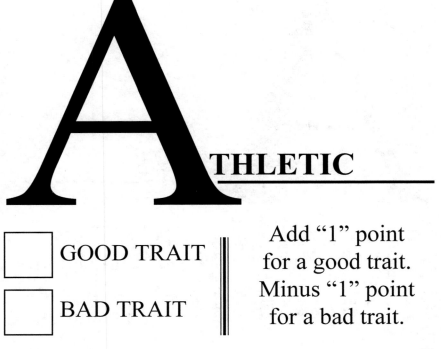

ATHLETIC

GOOD TRAIT

BAD TRAIT

Add "1" point for a good trait. Minus "1" point for a bad trait.

ACTIVE : Lively. Energetic.

MY ADVICE: You want this on your Mr. Right Wish List.
Why? Because he is the type who has more than one way to spend his free time, and it's not video games, bars, and other women.

- Choice: *can you live with this as a choice?*
- Character: *can you accept this is part of his character?*
- Compromise: *is this a trait you can compromise on?*
- Conform: *Can you help him conform this behavior?*
- Compatibility: *Do you have the same or similar trait?*
- Challenge: *Can you teach this trait as learned behavior?*

Reminder: The purpose is to create your Mr. Right Wish List.

GOOD TRAIT

BAD TRAIT

Add "1" point for a good trait.
Minus "1" point for a bad trait.

ATYPICAL : Nonconforming. Uncharacteristic.

MY ADVICE: You "do not" want this on your Mr. Right Wish List.
Why? Because he's the type that believes men come from mars and
women emerged from Venus, and that's all there is to it.

- Choice: *can you live with this as a choice?*
- Character: *can you accept this is part of his character?*
- Compromise: *is this a trait you can compromise on?*
- Conform: *Can you help him conform this behavior?*
- Compatibility: *Do you have the same or similar trait?*
- Challenge: *Can you teach this trait as learned behavior?*

> **Reminder: The purpose is to create your Mr. Right Wish List.**

TYPICAL

☐ GOOD TRAIT

☐ BAD TRAIT

Add "1" point
for a good trait.
Minus "1" point
for a bad trait.

ARCHIVAL: Sentimental. Saves for rainy days.

MY ADVICE: You want this on your Mr. Right Wish List.
Why? Because he is the type to value and appreciate things you do for him, say to him, and will hold on to gifts, cards, letters, savings, etc.

- Choice: *can you live with this as a choice?*
- Character: *can you accept this is part of his character?*
- Compromise: *is this a trait you can compromise on?*
- Conform: *Can you help him conform this behavior?*
- Compatibility: *Do you have the same or similar trait?*
- Challenge: *Can you teach this trait as learned behavior?*

Reminder: The purpose is to create your Mr. Right Wish List.

A RCHIVAL

☐ GOOD TRAIT

☐ BAD TRAIT

Add "1" point for a good trait. Minus "1" point for a bad trait.

ASSISTING : Supplementary. Supporting.

MY ADVICE: You want this on your Mr. Right Wish List.
Why? Because he is the type to help you and others without being asked just because he sees you need it.

- Choice: *can you live with this as a choice?*
- Character: *can you accept this is part of his character?*
- Compromise: *is this a trait you can compromise on?*
- Conform: *Can you help him conform this behavior?*
- Compatibility: *Do you have the same or similar trait?*
- Challenge: *Can you teach this trait as learned behavior?*

> **Reminder: The purpose is to create your Mr. Right Wish List.**

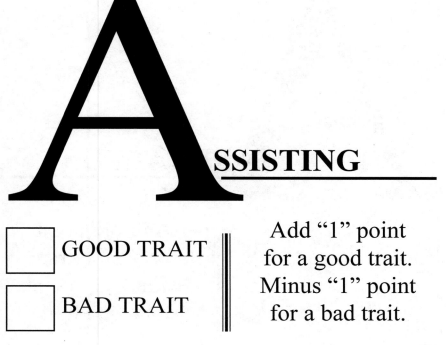

SSISTING

☐ GOOD TRAIT

☐ BAD TRAIT

Add "1" point for a good trait. Minus "1" point for a bad trait.

ANIMATED : Vibrant. Enthusiastic.

MY ADVICE: You want this on your Mr. Right Wish List.
Why? Because he is energetic, full of life, and has a wonderful sense
of humor and being able to find some laughter even in pain.

- Choice: *can you live with this as a choice?*
- Character: *can you accept this is part of his character?*
- Compromise: *is this a trait you can compromise on?*
- Conform: *Can you help him conform this behavior?*
- Compatibility: *Do you have the same or similar trait?*
- Challenge: *Can you teach this trait as learned behavior?*

Reminder: The purpose is to create your Mr. Right Wish List.

GOOD TRAIT

BAD TRAIT

Add "1" point
for a good trait.
Minus "1" point
for a bad trait.

ARCHEOLOGICAL : Supplementary. Supporting.

MY ADVICE: You want this on your Mr. Right Wish List.
Why? Because he is the type to help you and others without being
asked just because he sees you need it.

- Choice: *can you live with this as a choice?*
- Character: *can you accept this is part of his character?*
- Compromise: *is this a trait you can compromise on?*
- Conform: *Can you help him conform this behavior?*
- Compatibility: *Do you have the same or similar trait?*
- Challenge: *Can you teach this trait as learned behavior?*

Reminder: The purpose is to create your Mr. Right Wish List.

□ GOOD TRAIT

□ BAD TRAIT

Add "1" point
for a good trait.
Minus "1" point
for a bad trait.

ANTISOCIAL : Inconsiderate. Selfish.

MY ADVICE: You "do not" want this on your Mr. Right Wish List.
Why? Because he is a loner, and the type that even in a relationship
with you, places more value on being away from you.

- Choice: *can you live with this as a choice?*
- Character: *can you accept this is part of his character?*
- Compromise: *is this a trait you can compromise on?*
- Conform: *Can you help him conform this behavior?*
- Compatibility: *Do you have the same or similar trait?*
- Challenge: *Can you teach this trait as learned behavior?*

Reminder: The purpose is to create your Mr. Right Wish List.

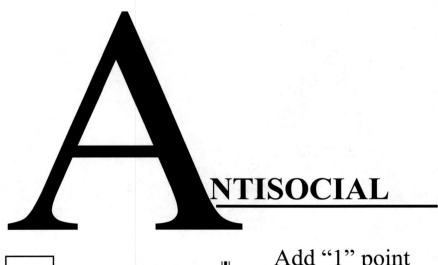

☐ GOOD TRAIT

☐ BAD TRAIT

Add "1" point
for a good trait.
Minus "1" point
for a bad trait.

APT: Suitable. Fitting.

MY ADVICE: You want this on your Mr. Right Wish List.
Why? Because he is capable of taking care of himself, and you. And won't tolerate living with his mom, or you taking care of him.

• Choice: *can you live with this as a choice?*
• Character: *can you accept this is part of his character?*
• Compromise: *is this a trait you can compromise on?*
• Conform: *Can you help him conform this behavior?*
• Compatibility: *Do you have the same or similar trait?*
• Challenge: *Can you teach this trait as learned behavior?*

Reminder: The purpose is to create your Mr. Right Wish List.

☐ GOOD TRAIT

☐ BAD TRAIT

Add "1" point
for a good trait.
Minus "1" point
for a bad trait.

ACRIMONIOUS : Bitter. Spiteful. Hostile.

MY ADVICE: You "do not" want this on your Mr. Right Wish List. Why? Because he is the type that has revenge in his heart with the sneaky, do things behind your back, personality to match.

- Choice: *can you live with this as a choice?*
- Character: *can you accept this is part of his character?*
- Compromise: *is this a trait you can compromise on?*
- Conform: *Can you help him conform this behavior?*
- Compatibility: *Do you have the same or similar trait?*
- Challenge: *Can you teach this trait as learned behavior?*

Reminder: The purpose is to create your Mr. Right Wish List.

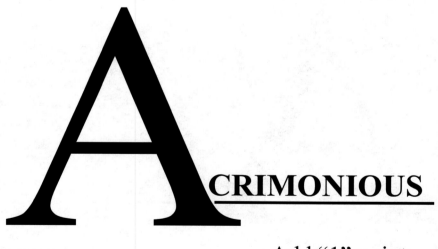

ACRIMONIOUS

☐ GOOD TRAIT

☐ BAD TRAIT

Add "1" point for a good trait. Minus "1" point for a bad trait.

ABLE : Capable. Talented. Gifted.

MY ADVICE: You want this on your Mr. Right Wish List.
Why? Because he is the type that does things to you that you've never experienced, and keeps you coming back for more.

- Choice: *can you live with this as a choice?*
- Character: *can you accept this is part of his character?*
- Compromise: *is this a trait you can compromise on?*
- Conform: *Can you help him conform this behavior?*
- Compatibility: *Do you have the same or similar trait?*
- Challenge: *Can you teach this trait as learned behavior?*

Reminder: The purpose is to create your Mr. Right Wish List.

ABLE _____

☐ GOOD TRAIT

☐ BAD TRAIT

Add "1" point for a good trait.
Minus "1" point for a bad trait.

ADORING : Tender. Doting. Warm.

MY ADVICE: You want this on your Mr. Right Wish List.
Why? Because he is the type to be romantic above all else. And
fawns over you in private and in public.

- Choice: *can you live with this as a choice?*
- Character: *can you accept this is part of his character?*
- Compromise: *is this a trait you can compromise on?*
- Conform: *Can you help him conform this behavior?*
- Compatibility: *Do you have the same or similar trait?*
- Challenge: *Can you teach this trait as learned behavior?*

Reminder: The purpose is to create your Mr. Right Wish List.

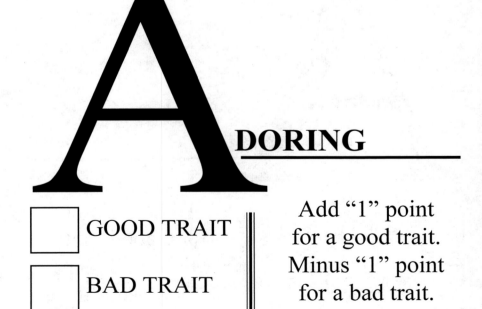

GOOD TRAIT

BAD TRAIT

Add "1" point
for a good trait.
Minus "1" point
for a bad trait.

ADORABLE : Sweet. Delightful. Endearing.

MY ADVICE: You want this on your Mr. Right Wish List.
Why? Because he is charming, gorgeous, and lovable. And has a whole list of qualities that make you fawn over him.

- Choice: *can you live with this as a choice?*
- Character: *can you accept this is part of his character?*
- Compromise: *is this a trait you can compromise on?*
- Conform: *Can you help him conform this behavior?*
- Compatibility: *Do you have the same or similar trait?*
- Challenge: *Can you teach this trait as learned behavior?*

Reminder: The purpose is to create your Mr. Right Wish List.

DORABLE

☐ GOOD TRAIT

☐ BAD TRAIT

Add "1" point for a good trait.
Minus "1" point for a bad trait.

ACRONYMED : Immature. Childish.

MY ADVICE: You "do not" want this on your Mr. Right Wish List. Why? Because he is the type that uses bff, omg, and lol much, much more than any normal well adjusted man would.

- Choice: *can you live with this as a choice?*
- Character: *can you accept this is part of his character?*
- Compromise: *is this a trait you can compromise on?*
- Conform: *Can you help him conform this behavior?*
- Compatibility: *Do you have the same or similar trait?*
- Challenge: *Can you teach this trait as learned behavior?*

Reminder: The purpose is to create your Mr. Right Wish List.

☐ GOOD TRAIT

☐ BAD TRAIT

Add "1" point for a good trait.
Minus "1" point for a bad trait.

ADJUSTED : Stable. Grounded.

MY ADVICE: You want this on your Mr. Right Wish List.
Why? Because he already has a career, and an active life that will blend or merge smoothly with yours.

- Choice: *can you live with this as a choice?*
- Character: *can you accept this is part of his character?*
- Compromise: *is this a trait you can compromise on?*
- Conform: *Can you help him conform this behavior?*
- Compatibility: *Do you have the same or similar trait?*
- Challenge: *Can you teach this trait as learned behavior?*

Reminder: The purpose is to create your Mr. Right Wish List.

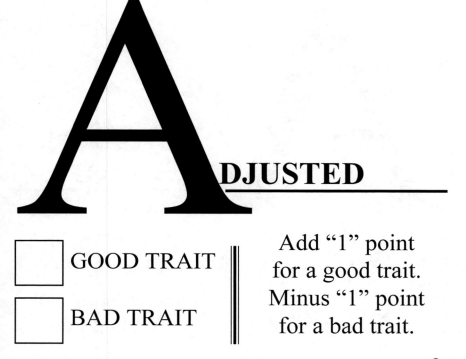

DJUSTED

□ GOOD TRAIT

□ BAD TRAIT

Add "1" point
for a good trait.
Minus "1" point
for a bad trait.

ATTITUDAL : Negative. Depressing. Pessimistic.

MY ADVICE: You "do not" want this on your Mr. Right Wish List.
Why? Because he is the type that always seems to have a bad day, no
matter how good things seem to be going around him.

- Choice: *can you live with this as a choice?*
- Character: *can you accept this is part of his character?*
- Compromise: *is this a trait you can compromise on?*
- Conform: *Can you help him conform this behavior?*
- Compatibility: *Do you have the same or similar trait?*
- Challenge: *Can you teach this trait as learned behavior?*

Reminder: The purpose is to create your Mr. Right Wish List.

$\square$ GOOD TRAIT

$\square$ BAD TRAIT

Add "1" point
for a good trait.
Minus "1" point
for a bad trait.

ANTICLIMACTIC : Gloomy. Cynical.

MY ADVICE: You "do not" want this on your Mr. Right Wish List. Why? Because he is the type to always look for and find the worst in everything and everyone. Without trying, he can spoil an orgasm.

- Choice: *can you live with this as a choice?*
- Character: *can you accept this is part of his character?*
- Compromise: *is this a trait you can compromise on?*
- Conform: *Can you help him conform this behavior?*
- Compatibility: *Do you have the same or similar trait?*
- Challenge: *Can you teach this trait as learned behavior?*

Reminder: The purpose is to create your Mr. Right Wish List.

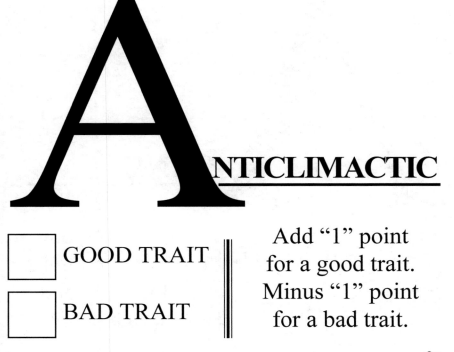

□ GOOD TRAIT

□ BAD TRAIT

Add "1" point for a good trait. Minus "1" point for a bad trait.

ASININE : Silly. Foolish. Idiotic.

MY ADVICE: You "do not" want this on your Mr. Right Wish List. Why? Because he is the type that always seem to say the wrong things, and still wants to be the center of attention.

- Choice: *can you live with this as a choice?*
- Character: *can you accept this is part of his character?*
- Compromise: *is this a trait you can compromise on?*
- Conform: *Can you help him conform this behavior?*
- Compatibility: *Do you have the same or similar trait?*
- Challenge: *Can you teach this trait as learned behavior?*

Reminder: The purpose is to create your Mr. Right Wish List.

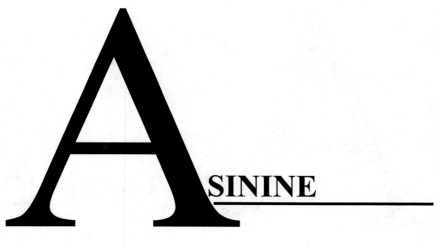

GOOD TRAIT

BAD TRAIT

Add "1" point for a good trait. Minus "1" point for a bad trait.

ALTERABLE : Open to change.

MY ADVICE: You want this on your Mr. Right Wish List.
Why? Because he is the type that isn't set in his ways and is open to seeing how things can be done differently, or better.

- Choice: *can you live with this as a choice?*
- Character: *can you accept this is part of his character?*
- Compromise: *is this a trait you can compromise on?*
- Conform: *Can you help him conform this behavior?*
- Compatibility: *Do you have the same or similar trait?*
- Challenge: *Can you teach this trait as learned behavior?*

> *Reminder: The purpose is to create your Mr. Right Wish List.*

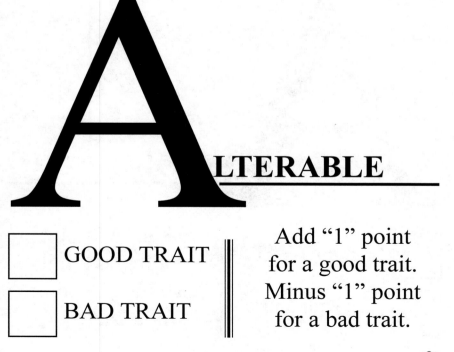

☐ GOOD TRAIT

☐ BAD TRAIT

Add "1" point for a good trait. Minus "1" point for a bad trait.

A**HOLE : Too many adjectives to list.

MY ADVICE: You "do not" want this on your Mr. Right Wish List. Why? Because he is the type that believes his feelings are all that matters. And if you've had to call him this on more than one occasion, things may only get worse.

- Choice: *can you live with this as a choice?*
- Character: *can you accept this is part of his character?*
- Compromise: *is this a trait you can compromise on?*
- Conform: *Can you help him conform this behavior?*
- Compatibility: *Do you have the same or similar trait?*
- Challenge: *Can you teach this trait as learned behavior?*

> **Reminder: The purpose is to create your Mr. Right Wish List.**

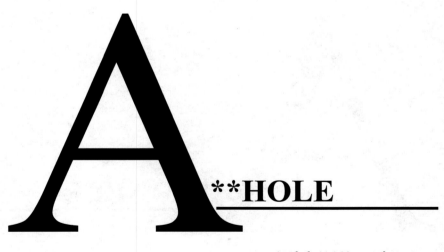

☐ GOOD TRAIT

☐ BAD TRAIT

Add "1" point for a good trait. Minus "1" point for a bad trait.

ASSESSING : Reviewing. Evaluating.

MY ADVICE: You want this on your Mr. Right Wish List.
Why? Because he is the type to look at all options first before he makes major decisions or provides a solution.

- Choice: *can you live with this as a choice?*
- Character: *can you accept this is part of his character?*
- Compromise: *is this a trait you can compromise on?*
- Conform: *Can you help him conform this behavior?*
- Compatibility: *Do you have the same or similar trait?*
- Challenge: *Can you teach this trait as learned behavior?*

Reminder: The purpose is to create your Mr. Right Wish List.

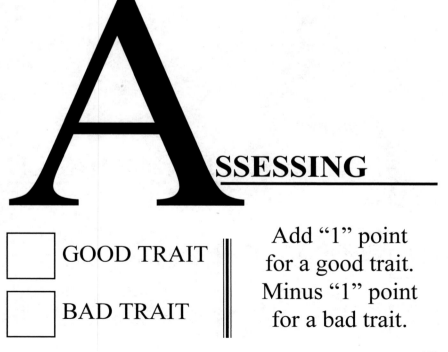

SSESSING

☐ GOOD TRAIT

☐ BAD TRAIT

Add "1" point for a good trait.
Minus "1" point for a bad trait.

APPROACHABLE : Open. Accessible.

MY ADVICE: You "do not" want this on your Mr. Right Wish List. Why? Because this may seem to be a good trait, but here's why it's not. If he's approachable by other women, he's not really yours.

- Choice: *can you live with this as a choice?*
- Character: *can you accept this is part of his character?*
- Compromise: *is this a trait you can compromise on?*
- Conform: *Can you help him conform this behavior?*
- Compatibility: *Do you have the same or similar trait?*
- Challenge: *Can you teach this trait as learned behavior?*

Reminder: The purpose is to create your Mr. Right Wish List.

PPROACHABLE

GOOD TRAIT

BAD TRAIT

Add "1" point for a good trait. Minus "1" point for a bad trait.

ALONE : Loner. Unattached.

MY ADVICE: You "do not" want this on your Mr. Right Wish List. Why? Because he is the type that if he's comfortable being a loner, and to himself, then he may never be satisfied even being with you.

- Choice: *can you live with this as a choice?*
- Character: *can you accept this is part of his character?*
- Compromise: *is this a trait you can compromise on?*
- Conform: *Can you help him conform this behavior?*
- Compatibility: *Do you have the same or similar trait?*
- Challenge: *Can you teach this trait as learned behavior?*

> **Reminder: The purpose is to create your Mr. Right Wish List.**

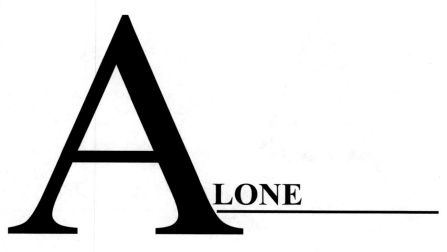

☐ GOOD TRAIT

☐ BAD TRAIT

Add "1" point for a good trait. Minus "1" point for a bad trait.

ALTARABLE : Committed. Ready.

MY ADVICE: You want this on your Mr. Right Wish List.
Why? Because he is the type that's not only willing to meet your mom, but is also ready to meet you at the Altar.

- Choice: *can you live with this as a choice?*
- Character: *can you accept this is part of his character?*
- Compromise: *is this a trait you can compromise on?*
- Conform: *Can you help him conform this behavior?*
- Compatibility: *Do you have the same or similar trait?*
- Challenge: *Can you teach this trait as learned behavior?*

Reminder: The purpose is to create your Mr. Right Wish List.

☐ GOOD TRAIT

☐ BAD TRAIT

Add "1" point for a good trait. Minus "1" point for a bad trait.

ADMIRABLE : Worthy. Highly Regarded.

MY ADVICE: You want this on your Mr. Right Wish List.
Why? Because he is the type that has qualities, gifts, talents, skills and abilities you don't see in other man, even several men combined.

- Choice: *can you live with this as a choice?*
- Character: *can you accept this is part of his character?*
- Compromise: *is this a trait you can compromise on?*
- Conform: *Can you help him conform this behavior?*
- Compatibility: *Do you have the same or similar trait?*
- Challenge: *Can you teach this trait as learned behavior?*

Reminder: The purpose is to create your Mr. Right Wish List.

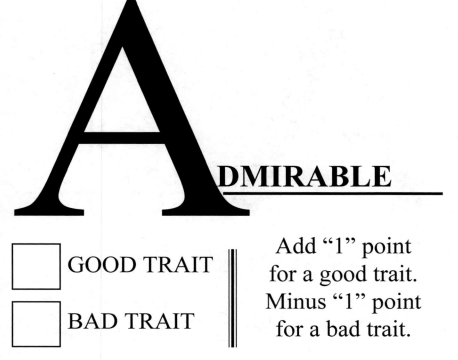

DMIRABLE

☐ GOOD TRAIT

☐ BAD TRAIT

Add "1" point for a good trait. Minus "1" point for a bad trait.

ANCIENT : Antique. Outdated. Antiquated.

MY ADVICE: You "do not" want this on your Mr. Right Wish List. Why? Because he isn't old fashioned, his ways, thoughts, ideals, are so beyond reason or reality that you can't deal with them.

- Choice: *can you live with this as a choice?*
- Character: *can you accept this is part of his character?*
- Compromise: *is this a trait you can compromise on?*
- Conform: *Can you help him conform this behavior?*
- Compatibility: *Do you have the same or similar trait?*
- Challenge: *Can you teach this trait as learned behavior?*

Reminder: The purpose is to create your Mr. Right Wish List.

GOOD TRAIT

BAD TRAIT

Add "1" point for a good trait. Minus "1" point for a bad trait.

AORTIVE : Compassionate. Kind. Giving.

MY ADVICE: You want this on your Mr. Right Wish List.
Why? Because he is the type that has a heart of gold, with you, his family, and others in need as well.

* Choice: *can you live with this as a choice?*
* Character: *can you accept this is part of his character?*
* Compromise: *is this a trait you can compromise on?*
* Conform: *Can you help him conform this behavior?*
* Compatibility: *Do you have the same or similar trait?*
* Challenge: *Can you teach this trait as learned behavior?*

Reminder: The purpose is to create your Mr. Right Wish List.

AORTIVE

☐ GOOD TRAIT

☐ BAD TRAIT

Add "1" point for a good trait. Minus "1" point for a bad trait.

APOLOGETIC : Repentant. Remorseful.

MY ADVICE: You want this on your Mr. Right Wish List.
Why? Because he is the type that always admits when he's wrong, and is willing to say so to you and others.

- Choice: *can you live with this as a choice?*
- Character: *can you accept this is part of his character?*
- Compromise: *is this a trait you can compromise on?*
- Conform: *Can you help him conform this behavior?*
- Compatibility: *Do you have the same or similar trait?*
- Challenge: *Can you teach this trait as learned behavior?*

Reminder: The purpose is to create your Mr. Right Wish List.

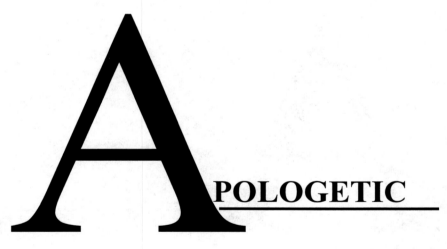

☐ GOOD TRAIT

☐ BAD TRAIT

Add "1" point
for a good trait.
Minus "1" point
for a bad trait.

ALL THAT : Too Many Adjectives To List.

MY ADVICE: You "do not" want this on your Mr. Right Wish List. Why? Because any man who believes he is all that, carries that god's gift to women mentality, therefore, he won't be satisfied with just you.

• Choice: *can you live with this as a choice?*
• Character: *can you accept this is part of his character?*
• Compromise: *is this a trait you can compromise on?*
• Conform: *Can you help him conform this behavior?*
• Compatibility: *Do you have the same or similar trait?*
• Challenge: *Can you teach this trait as learned behavior?*

Reminder: The purpose is to create your Mr. Right Wish List.

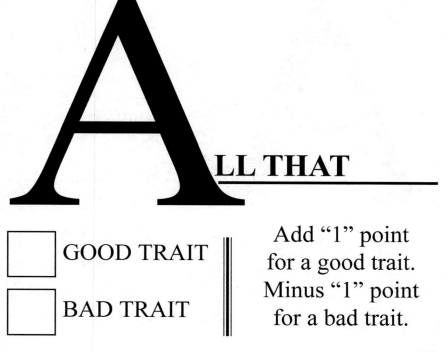

☐ GOOD TRAIT

☐ BAD TRAIT

Add "1" point for a good trait. Minus "1" point for a bad trait.

A-ONE : Admired. Sought After.

MY ADVICE: You want this on your Mr. Right Wish List.
Why? Because he is the type that many people admire, look up to, and is always on top of just about everything he does.

- Choice: *can you live with this as a choice?*
- Character: *can you accept this is part of his character?*
- Compromise: *is this a trait you can compromise on?*
- Conform: *Can you help him conform this behavior?*
- Compatibility: *Do you have the same or similar trait?*
- Challenge: *Can you teach this trait as learned behavior?*

Reminder: The purpose is to create your Mr. Right Wish List.

☐ GOOD TRAIT

☐ BAD TRAIT

Add "1" point for a good trait.
Minus "1" point for a bad trait.

AROMATIC : Masculine. Husky.

MY ADVICE: You want this on your Mr. Right Wish List.
Why? Because he has an intoxicating scent that you smell even when you're not around him, and that colognes simply enhance.

- Choice: *can you live with this as a choice?*
- Character: *can you accept this is part of his character?*
- Compromise: *is this a trait you can compromise on?*
- Conform: *Can you help him conform this behavior?*
- Compatibility: *Do you have the same or similar trait?*
- Challenge: *Can you teach this trait as learned behavior?*

Reminder: The purpose is to create your Mr. Right Wish List.

AROMATIC

☐ GOOD TRAIT

☐ BAD TRAIT

Add "1" point
for a good trait.
Minus "1" point
for a bad trait.

AFTERWARD : Thoughtful. Respectful.

MY ADVICE: You want this on your Mr. Right Wish List.
Why? Because he is the type that after sex, doesn't make a beeline for the bathroom, his clothes, and the door.

- Choice: *can you live with this as a choice?*
- Character: *can you accept this is part of his character?*
- Compromise: *is this a trait you can compromise on?*
- Conform: *Can you help him conform this behavior?*
- Compatibility: *Do you have the same or similar trait?*
- Challenge: *Can you teach this trait as learned behavior?*

Reminder: The purpose is to create your Mr. Right Wish List.

GOOD TRAIT

BAD TRAIT

Add "1" point for a good trait.
Minus "1" point for a bad trait.

AWARDED : Recognized. Acknowledged.

MY ADVICE: You want this on your Mr. Right Wish List.
Why? Because he's the type that does positive things that other people acknowledge, reward, and provided accolades to him for.

- Choice: *can you live with this as a choice?*
- Character: *can you accept this is part of his character?*
- Compromise: *is this a trait you can compromise on?*
- Conform: *Can you help him conform this behavior?*
- Compatibility: *Do you have the same or similar trait?*
- Challenge: *Can you teach this trait as learned behavior?*

Reminder: The purpose is to create your Mr. Right Wish List.

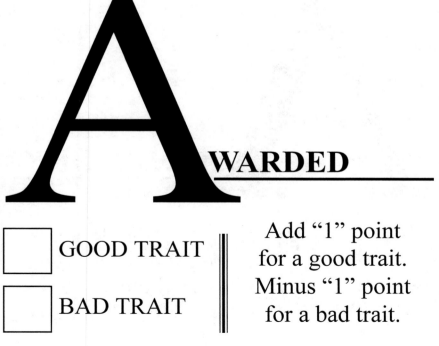

AWARDED

☐ GOOD TRAIT

☐ BAD TRAIT

Add "1" point
for a good trait.
Minus "1" point
for a bad trait.

ACCOLADING : Complementing. Congratulating.

MY ADVICE: You want this on your Mr. Right Wish List.
Why? Because he's the type that compliments you often and also
recognizes things you've done and rewards you for them.

- Choice: *can you live with this as a choice?*
- Character: *can you accept this is part of his character?*
- Compromise: *is this a trait you can compromise on?*
- Conform: *Can you help him conform this behavior?*
- Compatibility: *Do you have the same or similar trait?*
- Challenge: *Can you teach this trait as learned behavior?*

Reminder: The purpose is to create your Mr. Right Wish List.

A CCOLLADING

☐ GOOD TRAIT

☐ BAD TRAIT

Add "1" point
for a good trait.
Minus "1" point
for a bad trait.

ACCOMMODATING : Cooperative. Obliging.

MY ADVICE: You want this on your Mr. Right Wish List.
Why? Because he's the type that doesn't always have to have his
way, but gives you what you want at least 50% of the time.

- Choice: *can you live with this as a choice?*
- Character: *can you accept this is part of his character?*
- Compromise: *is this a trait you can compromise on?*
- Conform: *Can you help him conform this behavior?*
- Compatibility: *Do you have the same or similar trait?*
- Challenge: *Can you teach this trait as learned behavior?*

Reminder: The purpose is to create your Mr. Right Wish List.

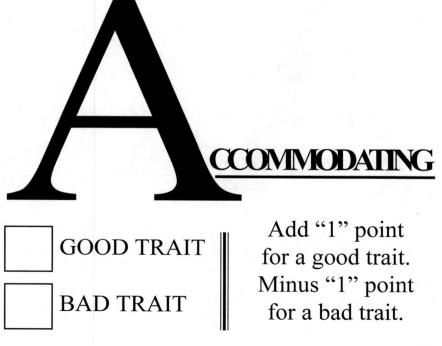

| GOOD TRAIT | Add "1" point for a good trait. |
| BAD TRAIT | Minus "1" point for a bad trait. |

ACTUAL : Genuine. Tangible.

MY ADVICE: You want this on your Mr. Right Wish List.
Why? Because he's the type that lives in the real world and doesn't waste time fantasizing or lying about things he does or what he has.

- Choice: *can you live with this as a choice?*
- Character: *can you accept this is part of his character?*
- Compromise: *is this a trait you can compromise on?*
- Conform: *Can you help him conform this behavior?*
- Compatibility: *Do you have the same or similar trait?*
- Challenge: *Can you teach this trait as learned behavior?*

Reminder: The purpose is to create your Mr. Right Wish List.

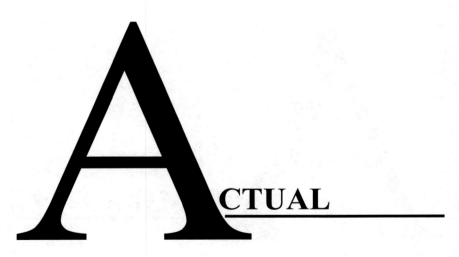

☐ GOOD TRAIT

☐ BAD TRAIT

Add "1" point for a good trait. Minus "1" point for a bad trait.

AERIAL : Hopeful. Optimistic.

MY ADVICE: You want this on your Mr. Right Wish List.
Why? Because he's the type that knows what he wants and follows his hopes and dreams by going after it; sees the sky and wants to reach it.

- Choice: *can you live with this as a choice?*
- Character: *can you accept this is part of his character?*
- Compromise: *is this a trait you can compromise on?*
- Conform: *Can you help him conform this behavior?*
- Compatibility: *Do you have the same or similar trait?*
- Challenge: *Can you teach this trait as learned behavior?*

Reminder: The purpose is to create your Mr. Right Wish List.

☐ **GOOD TRAIT**

☐ **BAD TRAIT**

Add "1" point
for a good trait.
Minus "1" point
for a bad trait.

AUTHENTIC : Genuine. Real.

MY ADVICE: You want this on your Mr. Right Wish List.
Why? Because he's the type that everything he says adds up. Even
the little details. And, even when you check behind him. This is rare.

- Choice: *can you live with this as a choice?*
- Character: *can you accept this is part of his character?*
- Compromise: *is this a trait you can compromise on?*
- Conform: *Can you help him conform this behavior?*
- Compatibility: *Do you have the same or similar trait?*
- Challenge: *Can you teach this trait as learned behavior?*

Reminder: The purpose is to create your Mr. Right Wish List.

AUTHENTIC

GOOD TRAIT

BAD TRAIT

Add "1" point
for a good trait.
Minus "1" point
for a bad trait.

ARGUABLE : Debatable.

MY ADVICE: You want this on your Mr. Right Wish List.
Why? Because he's the type that can have an adult conversation or disagreement without thinking he's always right.

• Choice: *can you live with this as a choice?*
• Character: *can you accept this is part of his character?*
• Compromise: *is this a trait you can compromise on?*
• Conform: *Can you help him conform this behavior?*
• Compatibility: *Do you have the same or similar trait?*
• Challenge: *Can you teach this trait as learned behavior?*

Reminder: The purpose is to create your Mr. Right Wish List.

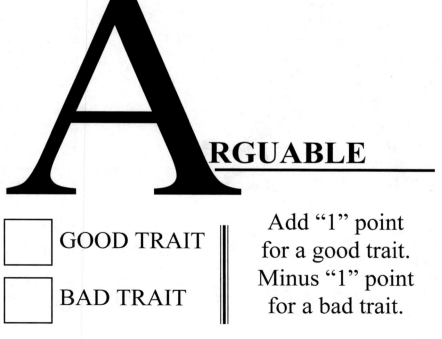

☐ GOOD TRAIT

☐ BAD TRAIT

Add "1" point for a good trait. Minus "1" point for a bad trait.

ADULT : Independent. Self-Reliant.

MY ADVICE: You want this on your Mr. Right Wish List.
Why? Because he's the type that has his own place, lives on his own, drives his own car, does his own laundry, and is an adult thinker.

- Choice: *can you live with this as a choice?*
- Character: *can you accept this is part of his character?*
- Compromise: *is this a trait you can compromise on?*
- Conform: *Can you help him conform this behavior?*
- Compatibility: *Do you have the same or similar trait?*
- Challenge: *Can you teach this trait as learned behavior?*

Reminder: The purpose is to create your Mr. Right Wish List.

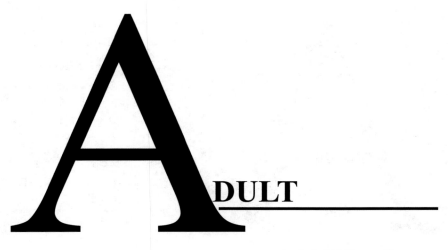

A**DULT**

GOOD TRAIT

BAD TRAIT

Add "1" point
for a good trait.
Minus "1" point
for a bad trait.

ACCREDITED : Endorsed. Certified.

MY ADVICE: You want this on your Mr. Right Wish List.
Why? Because he's the type that has a past that you don't have to help him hide or sweep under the rug. Thought well of by many others..

- Choice: *can you live with this as a choice?*
- Character: *can you accept this is part of his character?*
- Compromise: *is this a trait you can compromise on?*
- Conform: *Can you help him conform this behavior?*
- Compatibility: *Do you have the same or similar trait?*
- Challenge: *Can you teach this trait as learned behavior?*

> **Reminder: The purpose is to create your Mr. Right Wish List.**

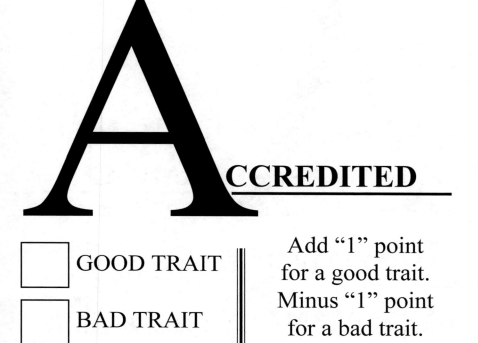

ACCREDITED

☐ GOOD TRAIT	Add "1" point for a good trait.
☐ BAD TRAIT	Minus "1" point for a bad trait.

ALARMING : Shocking. Upsetting.

MY ADVICE: You "do not" want this on your Mr. Right Wish List.
Why? Because he's the type that does or says things that make your
skin crawl, or the hairs on your neck stand up. Run...fast.

- Choice: *can you live with this as a choice?*
- Character: *can you accept this is part of his character?*
- Compromise: *is this a trait you can compromise on?*
- Conform: *Can you help him conform this behavior?*
- Compatibility: *Do you have the same or similar trait?*
- Challenge: *Can you teach this trait as learned behavior?*

Reminder: The purpose is to create your Mr. Right Wish List.

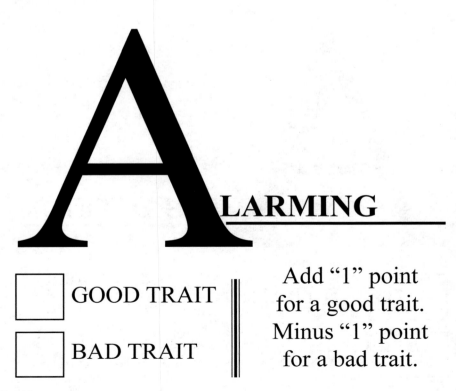

ALARMING

◻ GOOD TRAIT

◻ BAD TRAIT

Add "1" point
for a good trait.
Minus "1" point
for a bad trait.

AMBIDEXTROUS : Multifaceted. Multitasker.

MY ADVICE: You want this on your Mr. Right Wish List.
Why? Because he's able to use his left and right brain to think of
things to do to you in bed that will always keep you wanting more.

- Choice: *can you live with this as a choice?*
- Character: *can you accept this is part of his character?*
- Compromise: *is this a trait you can compromise on?*
- Conform: *Can you help him conform this behavior?*
- Compatibility: *Do you have the same or similar trait?*
- Challenge: *Can you teach this trait as learned behavior?*

Reminder: The purpose is to create your Mr. Right Wish List.

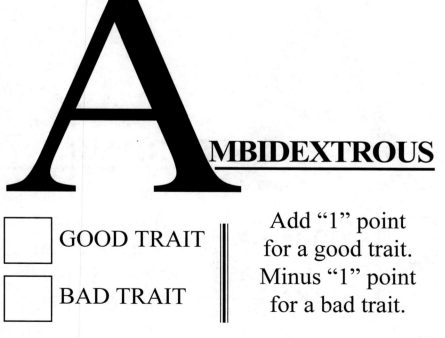

☐ GOOD TRAIT

☐ BAD TRAIT

Add "1" point
for a good trait.
Minus "1" point
for a bad trait.

AFFORDABLE : Reasonable. Inexpensive.

MY ADVICE: You want this on your Mr. Right Wish List.
Why? Because he's the type that will never go for you paying the
way for anything. And, can afford to have, keep and maintain you.

- Choice: *can you live with this as a choice?*
- Character: *can you accept this is part of his character?*
- Compromise: *is this a trait you can compromise on?*
- Conform: *Can you help him conform this behavior?*
- Compatibility: *Do you have the same or similar trait?*
- Challenge: *Can you teach this trait as learned behavior?*

Reminder: The purpose is to create your Mr. Right Wish List.

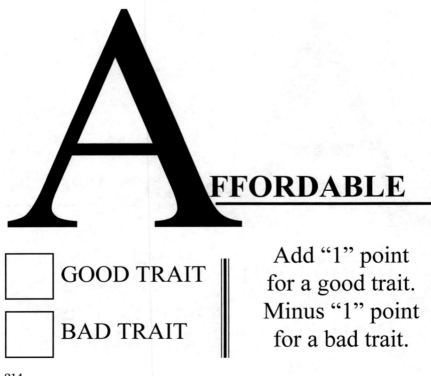

AFFORDABLE

☐ GOOD TRAIT

☐ BAD TRAIT

Add "1" point
for a good trait.
Minus "1" point
for a bad trait.

ANSWER-PRONE : Defensive. Unjustified.

MY ADVICE: You "do not" want this on your Mr. Right Wish List. Why? Because he's the type has an answer or excuse for everything, and nothing is ever his fault.

- Choice: *can you live with this as a choice?*
- Character: *can you accept this is part of his character?*
- Compromise: *is this a trait you can compromise on?*
- Conform: *Can you help him conform this behavior?*
- Compatibility: *Do you have the same or similar trait?*
- Challenge: *Can you teach this trait as learned behavior?*

Reminder: The purpose is to create your Mr. Right Wish List.

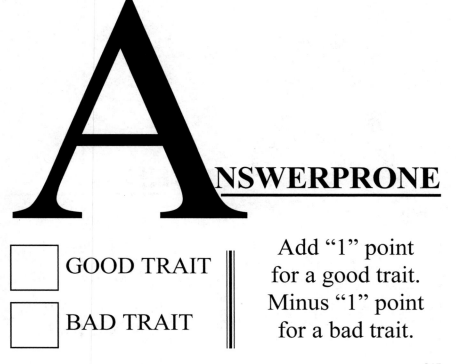

NSWERPRONE

☐ GOOD TRAIT

☐ BAD TRAIT

Add "1" point for a good trait. Minus "1" point for a bad trait.

ALLURING : Captivating. Fascinating.

MY ADVICE: You want this on your Mr. Right Wish List.
Why? Because he's the type that is just so sexy and dynamic that
you can't help but think about him, want him, and have to have him.

- Choice: *can you live with this as a choice?*
- Character: *can you accept this is part of his character?*
- Compromise: *is this a trait you can compromise on?*
- Conform: *Can you help him conform this behavior?*
- Compatibility: *Do you have the same or similar trait?*
- Challenge: *Can you teach this trait as learned behavior?*

Reminder: The purpose is to create your Mr. Right Wish List.

☐ GOOD TRAIT

☐ BAD TRAIT

Add "1" point
for a good trait.
Minus "1" point
for a bad trait.

AMENABLE : Willing to listen/learn. Open to Suggestion.

MY ADVICE: You want this on your Mr. Right Wish List.
Why? Because he's open to hearing his faults, and will welcome your like/dislike list without disagreeing with everything you point out.

- Choice: *can you live with this as a choice?*
- Character: *can you accept this is part of his character?*
- Compromise: *is this a trait you can compromise on?*
- Conform: *Can you help him conform this behavior?*
- Compatibility: *Do you have the same or similar trait?*
- Challenge: *Can you teach this trait as learned behavior?*

Reminder: The purpose is to create your Mr. Right Wish List.

☐ GOOD TRAIT

☐ BAD TRAIT

Add "1" point for a good trait. Minus "1" point for a bad trait.

ATTAINABLE : Reachable. Possible.

MY ADVICE: You want this on your Mr. Right Wish List.
Why? Because he's not your yet, but you see signs of light at the end of the tunnel, and he giving you signals that he's available.

- Choice: *can you live with this as a choice?*
- Character: *can you accept this is part of his character?*
- Compromise: *is this a trait you can compromise on?*
- Conform: *Can you help him conform this behavior?*
- Compatibility: *Do you have the same or similar trait?*
- Challenge: *Can you teach this trait as learned behavior?*

Reminder: The purpose is to create your Mr. Right Wish List.

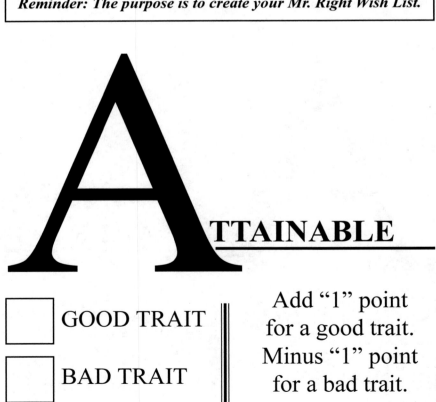

GOOD TRAIT

BAD TRAIT

Add "1" point
for a good trait.
Minus "1" point
for a bad trait.

AGING : Forward Thinking. Progressive.

MY ADVICE: You want this on your Mr. Right Wish List.
Why? Because he's the type that doesn't still live in the room he had in junior high. He grows in mind, body, spirit, and is very practical.

- Choice: *can you live with this as a choice?*
- Character: *can you accept this is part of his character?*
- Compromise: *is this a trait you can compromise on?*
- Conform: *Can you help him conform this behavior?*
- Compatibility: *Do you have the same or similar trait?*
- Challenge: *Can you teach this trait as learned behavior?*

Reminder: The purpose is to create your Mr. Right Wish List.

GING

☐ GOOD TRAIT

☐ BAD TRAIT

Add "1" point for a good trait.
Minus "1" point for a bad trait.

ARTISTIC : Creative. Resourceful.

MY ADVICE: You want this on your Mr. Right Wish List.
Why? Because he's the type that uses his imagination and skill both in his life, career, and in your bedroom, living room, kitchen, etc.

- Choice: *can you live with this as a choice?*
- Character: *can you accept this is part of his character?*
- Compromise: *is this a trait you can compromise on?*
- Conform: *Can you help him conform this behavior?*
- Compatibility: *Do you have the same or similar trait?*
- Challenge: *Can you teach this trait as learned behavior?*

Reminder: The purpose is to create your Mr. Right Wish List.

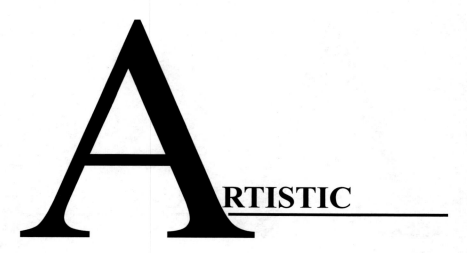

RTISTIC

☐ GOOD TRAIT

☐ BAD TRAIT

Add "1" point for a good trait. Minus "1" point for a bad trait.

AMORAL : Unscrupulous. Dishonorable.

MY ADVICE: You "do not" want this on your Mr. Right Wish List. Why? Because he's the type that will throw you under the bus and walk away without looking back just to save his own skin.

- Choice: *can you live with this as a choice?*
- Character: *can you accept this is part of his character?*
- Compromise: *is this a trait you can compromise on?*
- Conform: *Can you help him conform this behavior?*
- Compatibility: *Do you have the same or similar trait?*
- Challenge: *Can you teach this trait as learned behavior?*

> **Reminder: The purpose is to create your Mr. Right Wish List.**

☐ GOOD TRAIT

☐ BAD TRAIT

Add "1" point for a good trait. Minus "1" point for a bad trait.

AUDACIOUS : Bold. Brave.

MY ADVICE: You want this on your Mr. Right Wish List.
Why? Because he's the type that meets obstacles or hurdles head on
and has confidence that he can clear them and accomplish his task.

- Choice: *can you live with this as a choice?*
- Character: *can you accept this is part of his character?*
- Compromise: *is this a trait you can compromise on?*
- Conform: *Can you help him conform this behavior?*
- Compatibility: *Do you have the same or similar trait?*
- Challenge: *Can you teach this trait as learned behavior?*

> **Reminder: The purpose is to create your Mr. Right Wish List.**

UDACIOUS

☐ GOOD TRAIT

☐ BAD TRAIT

Add "1" point
for a good trait.
Minus "1" point
for a bad trait.

ABRAHAMIC : Conceited. Overconfident.

MY ADVICE: You "do not" want this on your Mr. Right Wish List.
Why? Because he wants to be the father of many nations; thinks he's
God's gift to women; has the kids and baby mama drama to prove it.

- Choice: *can you live with this as a choice?*
- Character: *can you accept this is part of his character?*
- Compromise: *is this a trait you can compromise on?*
- Conform: *Can you help him conform this behavior?*
- Compatibility: *Do you have the same or similar trait?*
- Challenge: *Can you teach this trait as learned behavior?*

Reminder: The purpose is to create your Mr. Right Wish List.

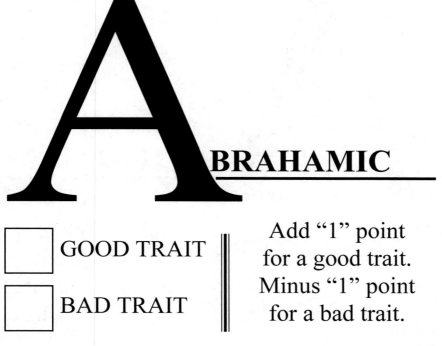

BRAHAMIC

☐ GOOD TRAIT

☐ BAD TRAIT

Add "1" point
for a good trait.
Minus "1" point
for a bad trait.

ARCHER : Unsettled. Fishing.

MY ADVICE: You "do not" want this on your Mr. Right Wish List. Why? Because he's the type who still has many arrows in his quiver pointed at you, and the bull's-eye of other women too.

- Choice: *can you live with this as a choice?*
- Character: *can you accept this is part of his character?*
- Compromise: *is this a trait you can compromise on?*
- Conform: *Can you help him conform this behavior?*
- Compatibility: *Do you have the same or similar trait?*
- Challenge: *Can you teach this trait as learned behavior?*

Reminder: The purpose is to create your Mr. Right Wish List.

ARCHER

☐ GOOD TRAIT

☐ BAD TRAIT

Add "1" point for a good trait. Minus "1" point for a bad trait.

ACCEPTED : Well Received. Appropriate.

MY ADVICE: You want this on your Mr. Right Wish List.
Why? Because he's the type that your mom, dad, priest, pastor, or other persons of significance believe is right for you.

- Choice: *can you live with this as a choice?*
- Character: *can you accept this is part of his character?*
- Compromise: *is this a trait you can compromise on?*
- Conform: *Can you help him conform this behavior?*
- Compatibility: *Do you have the same or similar trait?*
- Challenge: *Can you teach this trait as learned behavior?*

Reminder: The purpose is to create your Mr. Right Wish List.

ACCEPTED

GOOD TRAIT

BAD TRAIT

Add "1" point
for a good trait.
Minus "1" point
for a bad trait.

ABSORBING : Clingy. Engrossed.

MY ADVICE: You "do not" want this on your Mr. Right Wish List. Why? Because he's the type that takes everything in but never lets it out. And sponges, must release the water or they may explode.

- Choice: *can you live with this as a choice?*
- Character: *can you accept this is part of his character?*
- Compromise: *is this a trait you can compromise on?*
- Conform: *Can you help him conform this behavior?*
- Compatibility: *Do you have the same or similar trait?*
- Challenge: *Can you teach this trait as learned behavior?*

Reminder: The purpose is to create your Mr. Right Wish List.

GOOD TRAIT

BAD TRAIT

Add "1" point for a good trait. Minus "1" point for a bad trait.

ADULTERER : Cheat. Uncommitted.

MY ADVICE: You "do not" want this on your Mr. Right Wish List. Why? Because he says he's committed to you, but you find out he's still seeing someone else. One guess what happens if you marry him.

- Choice: *can you live with this as a choice?*
- Character: *can you accept this is part of his character?*
- Compromise: *is this a trait you can compromise on?*
- Conform: *Can you help him conform this behavior?*
- Compatibility: *Do you have the same or similar trait?*
- Challenge: *Can you teach this trait as learned behavior?*

Reminder: The purpose is to create your Mr. Right Wish List.

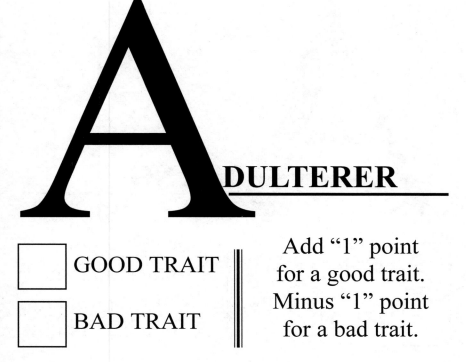

ADULTERER

☐ GOOD TRAIT

☐ BAD TRAIT

Add "1" point for a good trait. Minus "1" point for a bad trait.

ABIDING : Committed. Patient.

MY ADVICE: You want this on your Mr. Right Wish List.
Why? Because he's the type that starts and project and completes it.
And, is committed to whatever task he undertakes until it's done.

- Choice: *can you live with this as a choice?*
- Character: *can you accept this is part of his character?*
- Compromise: *is this a trait you can compromise on?*
- Conform: *Can you help him conform this behavior?*
- Compatibility: *Do you have the same or similar trait?*
- Challenge: *Can you teach this trait as learned behavior?*

Reminder: The purpose is to create your Mr. Right Wish List.

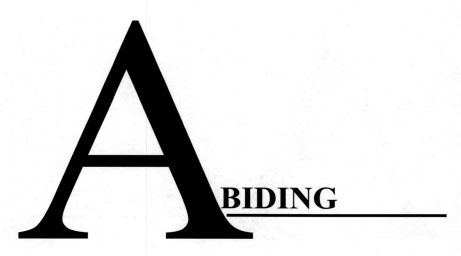

ABIDING

☐ GOOD TRAIT

☐ BAD TRAIT

Add "1" point
for a good trait.
Minus "1" point
for a bad trait.

ADVERSARIAL : Opposing. Anti.

MY ADVICE: You "do not" want this on your Mr. Right Wish List.
Why? Because he's the type to constantly go against everything you
say or do. Be careful, as this is a potential sign of a controlling trait.

- Choice: *can you live with this as a choice?*
- Character: *can you accept this is part of his character?*
- Compromise: *is this a trait you can compromise on?*
- Conform: *Can you help him conform this behavior?*
- Compatibility: *Do you have the same or similar trait?*
- Challenge: *Can you teach this trait as learned behavior?*

Reminder: The purpose is to create your Mr. Right Wish List.

ADVERSARIAL

GOOD TRAIT

BAD TRAIT

Add "1" point
for a good trait.
Minus "1" point
for a bad trait.

ADVOCATE : Supporter. Backer.

MY ADVICE: You want this on your Mr. Right Wish List.
Why? Because he's not only involved in social causes and changes,
he stands up for what is right.

- Choice: *can you live with this as a choice?*
- Character: *can you accept this is part of his character?*
- Compromise: *is this a trait you can compromise on?*
- Conform: *Can you help him conform this behavior?*
- Compatibility: *Do you have the same or similar trait?*
- Challenge: *Can you teach this trait as learned behavior?*

Reminder: The purpose is to create your Mr. Right Wish List.

GOOD TRAIT

BAD TRAIT

Add "1" point
for a good trait.
Minus "1" point
for a bad trait.

ALIVE : Upbeat. Thriving.

MY ADVICE: You want this on your Mr. Right Wish List.
Why? Because he's not the type to have a dry or dead or boring personality, and will keep things creative and exciting between you.

- Choice: *can you live with this as a choice?*
- Character: *can you accept this is part of his character?*
- Compromise: *is this a trait you can compromise on?*
- Conform: *Can you help him conform this behavior?*
- Compatibility: *Do you have the same or similar trait?*
- Challenge: *Can you teach this trait as learned behavior?*

Reminder: The purpose is to create your Mr. Right Wish List.

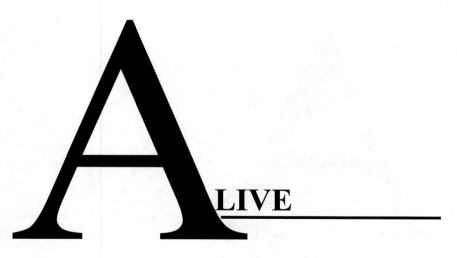

☐ GOOD TRAIT

☐ BAD TRAIT

Add "1" point for a good trait. Minus "1" point for a bad trait.

ASKABLE : Approachable. Considerate.

MY ADVICE: You want this on your Mr. Right Wish List.
Why? Because he's the type that is there when you need him. If you
have problems, concerns, questions, needs, you can depend on him.

- Choice: *can you live with this as a choice?*
- Character: *can you accept this is part of his character?*
- Compromise: *is this a trait you can compromise on?*
- Conform: *Can you help him conform this behavior?*
- Compatibility: *Do you have the same or similar trait?*
- Challenge: *Can you teach this trait as learned behavior?*

> **Reminder: The purpose is to create your Mr. Right Wish List.**

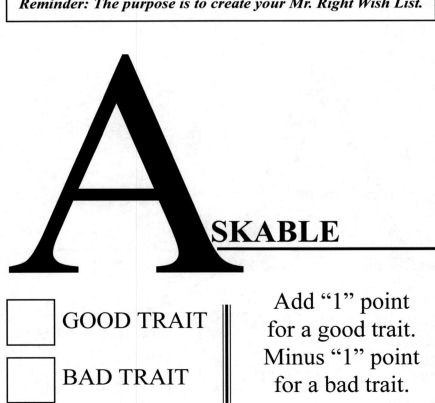

☐ GOOD TRAIT

☐ BAD TRAIT

Add "1" point
for a good trait.
Minus "1" point
for a bad trait.

ASSURED : Confident. Secure.

MY ADVICE: You want this on your Mr. Right Wish List.
Why? Because he is not only confident in himself, his sexuality, his
plans, hopes, dreams, etc., but is taking steps to meet them head on.

- Choice: *can you live with this as a choice?*
- Character: *can you accept this is part of his character?*
- Compromise: *is this a trait you can compromise on?*
- Conform: *Can you help him conform this behavior?*
- Compatibility: *Do you have the same or similar trait?*
- Challenge: *Can you teach this trait as learned behavior?*

Reminder: The purpose is to create your Mr. Right Wish List.

ASSURED

☐ GOOD TRAIT

☐ BAD TRAIT

Add "1" point
for a good trait.
Minus "1" point
for a bad trait.

ATONING : Repentant. Sorrowful.

MY ADVICE: You want this on your Mr. Right Wish List.
Why? Because he is the type to stand up and take responsibility for what he's done. And when he's wrong, he doesn't blame others.

- Choice: *can you live with this as a choice?*
- Character: *can you accept this is part of his character?*
- Compromise: *is this a trait you can compromise on?*
- Conform: *Can you help him conform this behavior?*
- Compatibility: *Do you have the same or similar trait?*
- Challenge: *Can you teach this trait as learned behavior?*

Reminder: The purpose is to create your Mr. Right Wish List.

GOOD TRAIT

BAD TRAIT

Add "1" point for a good trait.
Minus "1" point for a bad trait.

AUTHORITATIVE : One sided. Narrow Minded.

MY ADVICE: You "do not" want this on your Mr. Right Wish List. Why? Because he wants his way or no way. Head of household is one thing, but 'I'm the king of the castle' played out a long time ago.

- Choice: *can you live with this as a choice?*
- Character: *can you accept this is part of his character?*
- Compromise: *is this a trait you can compromise on?*
- Conform: *Can you help him conform this behavior?*
- Compatibility: *Do you have the same or similar trait?*
- Challenge: *Can you teach this trait as learned behavior?*

Reminder: The purpose is to create your Mr. Right Wish List.

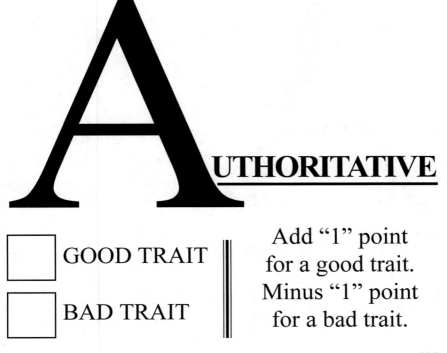

UTHORITATIVE

☐ GOOD TRAIT

☐ BAD TRAIT

Add "1" point for a good trait. Minus "1" point for a bad trait.

AUTHOR : Creative. Visionary.

MY ADVICE: You want this on your Mr. Right Wish List.
Why? Because he has imagination, creativity, and is always paving
new paths to success; and has many dynamic workable plans.

- Choice: *can you live with this as a choice?*
- Character: *can you accept this is part of his character?*
- Compromise: *is this a trait you can compromise on?*
- Conform: *Can you help him conform this behavior?*
- Compatibility: *Do you have the same or similar trait?*
- Challenge: *Can you teach this trait as learned behavior?*

Reminder: The purpose is to create your Mr. Right Wish List.

☐ GOOD TRAIT

☐ BAD TRAIT

Add "1" point
for a good trait.
Minus "1" point
for a bad trait.

AWAKE : Familiar. Knowledgeable.

MY ADVICE: You want this on your Mr. Right Wish List.
Why? Because he stays on top of current events and how things affect you, and knows more than the name of the latest video game.

• Choice: *can you live with this as a choice?*
• Character: *can you accept this is part of his character?*
• Compromise: *is this a trait you can compromise on?*
• Conform: *Can you help him conform this behavior?*
• Compatibility: *Do you have the same or similar trait?*
• Challenge: *Can you teach this trait as learned behavior?*

Reminder: The purpose is to create your Mr. Right Wish List.

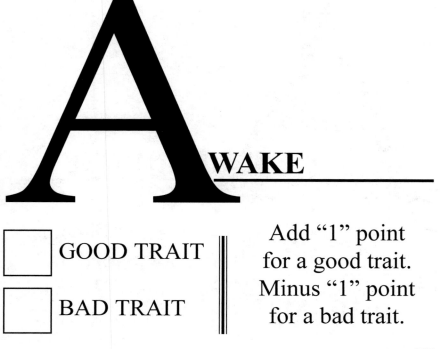

□ **GOOD TRAIT**

□ **BAD TRAIT**

Add "1" point for a good trait.
Minus "1" point for a bad trait.

ALTRUISTIC : Unselfish. Giving.

MY ADVICE: You want this on your Mr. Right Wish List.
Why? Because he's the type that puts your needs first, especially in bed. And, is a supporter or volunteer of all that is good and right.

- Choice: *can you live with this as a choice?*
- Character: *can you accept this is part of his character?*
- Compromise: *is this a trait you can compromise on?*
- Conform: *Can you help him conform this behavior?*
- Compatibility: *Do you have the same or similar trait?*
- Challenge: *Can you teach this trait as learned behavior?*

Reminder: The purpose is to create your Mr. Right Wish List.

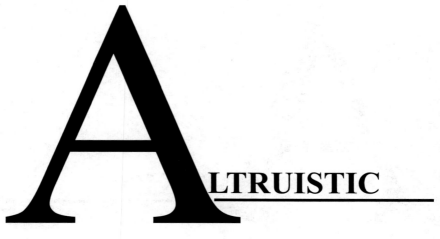

☐ GOOD TRAIT

☐ BAD TRAIT

Add "1" point for a good trait.
Minus "1" point for a bad trait.

ATTIRED : Wardrobed. Diverse.

MY ADVICE: You want this on your Mr. Right Wish List.
Why? Because he's the type that has more than just the shirt you bought him, and his team jersey in his closet, and understands why.

• Choice: *can you live with this as a choice?*
• Character: *can you accept this is part of his character?*
• Compromise: *is this a trait you can compromise on?*
• Conform: *Can you help him conform this behavior?*
• Compatibility: *Do you have the same or similar trait?*
• Challenge: *Can you teach this trait as learned behavior?*

Reminder: The purpose is to create your Mr. Right Wish List.

☐ GOOD TRAIT

☐ BAD TRAIT

Add "1" point for a good trait. Minus "1" point for a bad trait.

AFRAID : Fearful. Troubled.

MY ADVICE: You "do not" want this on your Mr. Right Wish List.
Why? Because he's scared to get back up and try again if he's experienced failure. If he's afraid to fail, he'll never achieve success.

- Choice: *can you live with this as a choice?*
- Character: *can you accept this is part of his character?*
- Compromise: *is this a trait you can compromise on?*
- Conform: *Can you help him conform this behavior?*
- Compatibility: *Do you have the same or similar trait?*
- Challenge: *Can you teach this trait as learned behavior?*

Reminder: The purpose is to create your Mr. Right Wish List.

GOOD TRAIT

BAD TRAIT

Add "1" point
for a good trait.
Minus "1" point
for a bad trait.

ACCOUNTABLE : Responsible. Answerable.

MY ADVICE: You want this on your Mr. Right Wish List.
Why? Because he says what he means and means what he says. The various areas of his life are balanced & your relationship will be too.

- Choice: *can you live with this as a choice?*
- Character: *can you accept this is part of his character?*
- Compromise: *is this a trait you can compromise on?*
- Conform: *Can you help him conform this behavior?*
- Compatibility: *Do you have the same or similar trait?*
- Challenge: *Can you teach this trait as learned behavior?*

Reminder: The purpose is to create your Mr. Right Wish List.

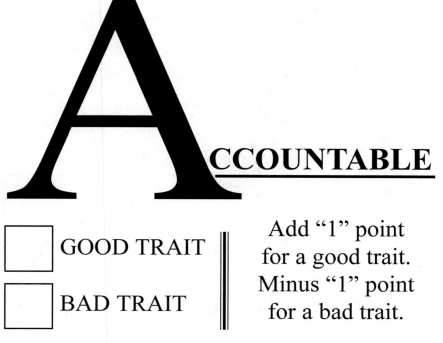

☐ GOOD TRAIT

☐ BAD TRAIT

Add "1" point for a good trait.
Minus "1" point for a bad trait.

ALCOHOLIC : Self Explanatory.

MY ADVICE: You "do not" want this on your Mr. Right Wish List. Why? Because the vast majority of men who are constantly and/or consistently under the influence of any substance, can be dangerous.

- Choice: *can you live with this as a choice?*
- Character: *can you accept this is part of his character?*
- Compromise: *is this a trait you can compromise on?*
- Conform: *Can you help him conform this behavior?*
- Compatibility: *Do you have the same or similar trait?*
- Challenge: *Can you teach this trait as learned behavior?*

Reminder: The purpose is to create your Mr. Right Wish List.

☐ GOOD TRAIT

☐ BAD TRAIT

Add "1" point for a good trait. Minus "1" point for a bad trait.

ADDICTED : Self-Explanatory.

MY ADVICE: You "do not" want this on your Mr. Right Wish List.
Why? Because addictions are often precursors to other unsavory behavior. If he can't function without his drug of choice, be careful.

- Choice: *can you live with this as a choice?*
- Character: *can you accept this is part of his character?*
- Compromise: *is this a trait you can compromise on?*
- Conform: *Can you help him conform this behavior?*
- Compatibility: *Do you have the same or similar trait?*
- Challenge: *Can you teach this trait as learned behavior?*

Reminder: The purpose is to create your Mr. Right Wish List.

GOOD TRAIT

BAD TRAIT

Add "1" point
for a good trait.
Minus "1" point
for a bad trait.

ABUSIVE : Self-Explanatory.

MY ADVICE: You "do not" want this on your Mr. Right Wish List. Why? Because if he is verbally, physically, hidden or publicly abusive toward you, and/or your kids, run and run fast.

- Choice: *can you live with this as a choice?*
- Character: *can you accept this is part of his character?*
- Compromise: *is this a trait you can compromise on?*
- Conform: *Can you help him conform this behavior?*
- Compatibility: *Do you have the same or similar trait?*
- Challenge: *Can you teach this trait as learned behavior?*

Reminder: The purpose is to create your Mr. Right Wish List.

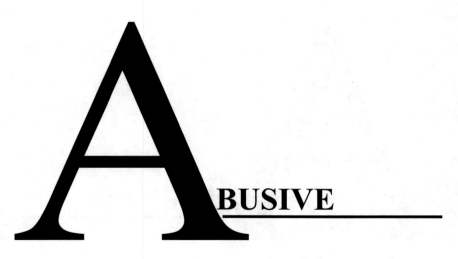

AFFLUENT : Settled. Comfortable.

MY ADVICE: You want this on your Mr. Right Wish List.
Why? Because even though money can never buy love or happiness,
it's a great foundation to start from. And, he won't need yours.

- Choice: *can you live with this as a choice?*
- Character: *can you accept this is part of his character?*
- Compromise: *is this a trait you can compromise on?*
- Conform: *Can you help him conform this behavior?*
- Compatibility: *Do you have the same or similar trait?*
- Challenge: *Can you teach this trait as learned behavior?*

Reminder: The purpose is to create your Mr. Right Wish List.

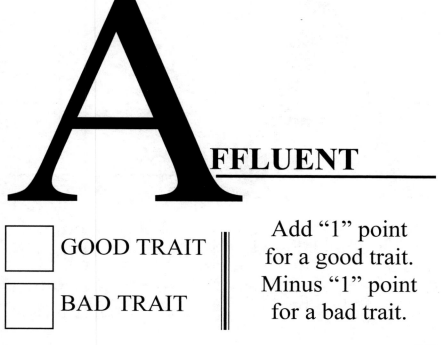

AFFLUENT

GOOD TRAIT

BAD TRAIT

Add "1" point
for a good trait.
Minus "1" point
for a bad trait.

AGLOW : Radiant. Glowing.

MY ADVICE: You want this on your Mr. Right Wish List.
Why? Because he lights up when he sees you. And you light up when you see him. If your heart skips a beat, he's a Keeper.

- Choice: *can you live with this as a choice?*
- Character: *can you accept this is part of his character?*
- Compromise: *is this a trait you can compromise on?*
- Conform: *Can you help him conform this behavior?*
- Compatibility: *Do you have the same or similar trait?*
- Challenge: *Can you teach this trait as learned behavior?*

Reminder: The purpose is to create your Mr. Right Wish List.

☐ GOOD TRAIT

☐ BAD TRAIT

Add "1" point for a good trait. Minus "1" point for a bad trait.

ARDENT : Focused. Zealous.

MY ADVICE: You want this on your Mr. Right Wish List.
Why? Because he's the type that stays committed to what he does,
and is likely to be devoted, committed, and dedicated to you as well.

- Choice: *can you live with this as a choice?*
- Character: *can you accept this is part of his character?*
- Compromise: *is this a trait you can compromise on?*
- Conform: *Can you help him conform this behavior?*
- Compatibility: *Do you have the same or similar trait?*
- Challenge: *Can you teach this trait as learned behavior?*

Reminder: The purpose is to create your Mr. Right Wish List.

GOOD TRAIT

BAD TRAIT

Add "1" point
for a good trait.
Minus "1" point
for a bad trait.

AGGRESSIVE : Violent. Hostile.

MY ADVICE: You "do not" want this on your Mr. Right Wish List. Why? Because he's the type that has a destructive, belligerent attitude, and it often escalates from anger, to violence, to revenge.

- Choice: *can you live with this as a choice?*
- Character: *can you accept this is part of his character?*
- Compromise: *is this a trait you can compromise on?*
- Conform: *Can you help him conform this behavior?*
- Compatibility: *Do you have the same or similar trait?*
- Challenge: *Can you teach this trait as learned behavior?*

Reminder: The purpose is to create your Mr. Right Wish List.

GGRESIVE

☐ GOOD TRAIT

☐ BAD TRAIT

Add "1" point
for a good trait.
Minus "1" point
for a bad trait.

AFTERBURNER : Wants to plant seeds in all the flowers.

MY ADVICE: You "do not" want this on your Mr. Right Wish List. Why? Because he's the type that you cannot afford to have sex with unless you want to feel the afterburn and be headed to the free clinic.

- Choice: *can you live with this as a choice?*
- Character: *can you accept this is part of his character?*
- Compromise: *is this a trait you can compromise on?*
- Conform: *Can you help him conform this behavior?*
- Compatibility: *Do you have the same or similar trait?*
- Challenge: *Can you teach this trait as learned behavior?*

Reminder: The purpose is to create your Mr. Right Wish List.

AFTERBURNER

☐ GOOD TRAIT

☐ BAD TRAIT

Add "1" point for a good trait. Minus "1" point for a bad trait.

BASIC RELATIONSHIP QUESTIONS
TO ASK YOURSELF

- Choice: *can you live with this as a choice?*
- Character: *can you accept this is part of his character?*
- Compromise: *is this a trait you can compromise on?*
- Conform: *Can you help him conform this behavior?*
- Compatibility: *Do you have the same or similar trait?*
- Challenge: *Can you teach this trait as learned behavior?*

CHAPTER NINE

CHART AND SCALE

CHART AND SCALE

The Benchmark of Measurable Results

Now that you know the 100 words selected to make up an **"A-LIST"** is your Mr. Right on it? Where does he fit? In the highest percentage? The lowest? Middle? Exactly where you want him? And how does he measure up to what you thought of him before you read this book?

If your Mr. Right has passed with flying colors, and after reading the material in this book, you've learned that he is actually a better person overall than you ever imagined him to be, first, give him credit for being more than you thought he was; and second, give yourself credit for taking the time to learn ways of determining that, and for noticing. Now, let's take it one step further:

1. You've been given the Course and the Challenge of teaching your Mr. Right how to be and stay romantic through the proven strategy of **Learned Behavior**.

2. You've been given a Romance Calendar, by which to help him learn to do certain things that you expect of him over a period of time, that can keep the romantic flame lit.

3. You've been given a List of 100 words that were compiled using three criteria of research, recollection, and recall, and can help you to determine just how good or bad your Mr. Right actually is.

And now...

4. We're going to measure the results of how your Mr. Right will do <u>after</u> a few months of actually doing the things you put on your Romance Calendar.

My suggestion to you is to measure the results every three months after you start your calendar. That way, you can see and gauge what works, what doesn't, what needs to be added, removed, modified, etc.

You can learn some valuable information about your Mr. Right's likes, dislikes, and willingness to please you even though he may not like something, simply by you measuring the Romance Results regularly.

A-LIST CHART AND SCALE

These 100 words that make up my sample A-List. You can use any words to make your own and a similar scale to measure results. This chart can help you learn more about your Mr. Right, identify character traits you didn't know he had, etc. However he scores, know that you can play a major role in helping to conform his character and behavior into what you want and need it to be.

						SCALE: 75%-100% = "A" | 50%-74% = "B" | 25%-49% = "C" | 0%-24% = "D".
1. Abject		34. Adoring		67. Answerprone		
2. Absolute		35. Adorable		68. Alluring		
3. Attentive		36. Acronymed		69. Amenable		
4. Attractive		37. Adjusted		70. Attainable		
5. Affectionate		38. Attitudal		71. Aging		
6. Adjustable		39. Anticlimactic		72. Artistic		
7. Absolving		40. Asinine		73. Amoral		
8. Adaptable		41. Alterable		74. Audacity		
9. Alpha		42. A**hole		75. Abrahamic		
10. Associated		43. Assessing		76. Archer		
11. Angelic		44. Approachable		77. Accepted		
12. Anatomical		45. Alone		78. Absorbing		
13. Au Jure		46. Altarable		79. Adulterer		
14. Architectural		47. Admirable		80. Abiding		
15. Average		48. Ancient		81. Adversarial		
16. Anointed		49. Aortive		82. Advocate		
17. Accepting		50. Apologetic		83. Alive		
18. Agreeable		51. All that		84. Askable		
19. Acknowledging		52. A-one		85. Assured		
20. Accordingly		53. Aromatic		86. Atoning		
21. Acting		54. Afterward		87. Authoritative		
22. Ascending		55. Awarded		88. Author		
23. Athletic		56. Accolading		89. Awake		
24. Active		57. Accommodating		90. Altruistic		
25. Atypical		58. Actual		91. Attired		
26. Archival		59. Aerial		92. Afraid		
27. Assisting		60. Authentic		93. Accountable		
28. Animated		61. Arguable		94. Alcoholic		
29. Archeological		62. Adult		95. Addicted		
30. Antisocial		63. Accredited		96. Abusive		
31. Apt		64. Alarming		97. Affluent		
32. A danger		65. Ambidextrous		98. Aglow		
33. Able		66. Affordable		99. Ardent		
				100. Aggressive		

Add up the total number from 1 to 100. <u>How did he score?</u>
Mark "+1 or -1" point in each box that represents your Mr. Right.

ROMANCE RESULTS CHART

Below, is my sample Romance List and a twelve-month timeline. Use this chart to identify whether or not your Mr. Right "did" the activity you placed on the Romance Calendar. Put an "X" in the box.

The chart can help you see where you are having success; areas that need more attention; what works during certain months; what you or he likes or doesn't like in certain seasons, etc.; and how open he actually is to participating in the proven strategy of treating romance as learned behavior. Have fun!

ROMANCE LIST	CALENDAR YEAR											
	1	2	3	4	5	6	7	8	9	10	11	12
1. Cuddled With Me												
2. Said I Love You												
3. Opened Doors For Me												
4. Held My Hand												
5. Touched Me Sensually												
6. Nustled My Neck												
7. Fixed Me Hot Baths												
8. Tongue Only Sexed Me												
9. Paid Attention To Me												
10. Candlelight Dined Me												
11. Romantic Weekended Me												
12. Danced With Me												
13. Spooned With Me												
14. Took Long Walks With Me												
15. Kissed Me Passionately												
16. Made Me Laugh												
17. Flirted With Me												
18. Licked My E-Zones												
19. Gave Me Massages												
20. Gave Me Foot Rubs												
21. Gave Me Toe Sucking												
22. Communicated With Me												
23. Listened To Me												
24. Gave Me Flowers, Gifts, Cards, Candy, and/or Poetry												
25. Took a Class With Me												

ROMANCE ASSESSMENT CHART

You can assess how willing, or unwilling Mr. Right was at beig romantic. Be honest. Don't say he was willing just because he did it, if he grumbled the entire time. You may be okay with your Mr. Right grumbling about a romance activity you placed on the calendar, "as long as he did it" but let me remind you, it's about "learned behavior". If he grumbles about one type of romance, he may grumble about all. Again, I suggest making your chart month by month for the year. Use three categories for each month. Here's an example.

Willing W	Grumbled G	Unwilling U	Place a 'W' - 'G' - or 'U' in the right box											
			CALENDAR YEAR												
ROMANCE LIST			1	2	3	4	5	6	7	8	9	10	11	12	ttl
1. Cuddled With Me															
2. Said I Love You															
3. Opened Doors For Me															
4. Held My Hand															
5. Touched Me Sensually															
6. Nustled My Neck															
7. Fixed Me Hot Baths															
8. Tongue Only Sexed Me															
9. Paid Attention To Me															
10. Candlelight Dined Me															
11. Romantic Weekended Me															
12. Danced With Me															
13. Spooned With Me															
14. Took Long Walks With Me															
15. Kissed Me Passionately															
16. Made Me Laugh															
17. Flirted With Me															
18. Licked My E-Zones															
19. Gave Me Massages															
20. Gave Me Foot Rubs															
21. Gave Me Toe Sucking															
22. Communicated With Me															
23. Listened To Me															
24. Gave Me Flowers, Gifts, Cards, Candy, and/or Poetry															
25. Took a Class With Me															

CHAPTER TEN

CLOSING THOUGHTS

CLOSING THOUGHTS

Sentimental Reasons versus Stark Reality

Teaching young boys **romance before reproduction** can help them learn to stop degrading young women, treating women like mere sex objects, rather than the queens and princesses they are. And, it can certainly help boys, grow into mature, respectful, romantic, men.

Women want their Mr. Right to be passionate, playful, powerful, persistent, paid up, and if at all possible…perfect. Those sentimental reasons are fine. But, the stark reality is that it takes some men longer than others to accomplish certain things. And, there are some other stark realities that can clear your thinking when it comes to looking for, or being in a relationship with Mr. Right. What that means, quite often, is that some of those stark realities may also include:

• How important faith is to him, and whether he puts it into action.
• How he treats you, is based on how others have treated him.
• How and where he grew up in his childhood.
• Any tragedy that may have occurred with, near, or around him.
• The causes and effects of his relationships with others.
  (whether he has lasting ones or has burned every bridge he built)
• Any negative influences in his life such as addictions, or crime.

Vital

How much 'non-sex' value he places on your relationship.

Men at certain ages, become set in their ways. However, teaching romance as a learned behavior crosses age lines, and there are still other stark realities that you may need to take into consideration before you start down this road with your Mr. Right.

They include:

1. Have you ever <u>asked</u> him **his** reasons for not being romantic?

2. Have you <u>asked</u> if he's willing to treat the art of romance more important and/or equal to act of reproduction?

3. Have you <u>asked</u> if he's willing to discuss a new, learned behavior?

Once these stark realities surface, and are dealt with, you can move forward in newness. And, you can often move forward without ever touching on these at all. All men are different. There is no miracle pill. But when men are willing, there can be **learned behavior**.

For anyone that tries to tell you that romance is not Biblical,

please point them to the book called Song of Solomon

A-List

1. Abject
2. Absolute
3. Attentive
4. Attractive
5. Affectionate
6. Adjustable
7. Absolving
8. Adaptable
9. Alpha
10. Associated
11. Angelic
12. Anatomical
13. Au Jure
14. Architectural
15. Average
16. Anointed
17. Accepting
18. Agreeable
19. Acknowledging
20. Accordingly
21. Acting
22. Ascending
23. Athletic
24. Active
25. Atypical
26. Archival
27. Assisting
28. Animated
29. Archeological
30. Antisocial
31. Apt
32. A danger
33. Able
34. Adoring
35. Adorable
36. Acronymed
37. Adjusted
38. Attitudal
39. Anticlimactic
40. Asinine
41. Alterable
42. A**hole
43. Assessing
44. Approachable
45. Alone
46. Altarable
47. Admirable
48. Ancient
49. Aortive
50. Apologetic
51. All that
52. A-one
53. Aromatic
54. Afterward
55. Awarded
56. Accolading
57. Accommodating
58. Actual
59. Aerial
60. Authentic
61. Arguable
62. Adult
63. Accredited
64. Alarming
65. Ambidextrous
66. Affordable
67. Answerprone
68. Alluring
69. Amenable
70. Attainable
71. Aging
72. Artistic
73. Amoral
74. Audacity
75. Abrahamic
76. Archer
77. Accepted
78. Absorbing
79. Adulterer
80. Abiding
81. Adversarial
82. Advocate
83. Alive
84. Askable
85. Assured
86. Atoning
87. Authoritative
88. Author
89. Awake
90. Altruistic
91. Attired
92. Afraid
93. Accountable
94. Alcoholic
95. Addicted
96. Abusive
97. Affluent
98. Aglow
99. Ardent
100. Aggressive

Note: Afterburn is not on this list because it is a bonus word.

Contact

Author: Keith Hammond
President
Lessons For Life Books, Inc.
7455 France Avenue South #305
Edina, MN 55435

(952) 884-5498 ofc
(952) 884-3785 fax

author@LessonsForLifeBooks.com

web: LessonsForLifeBooks.com

How to Find Us:

Google:
'keith hammond lessons for life books'

Barnes & Noble:
bn.com
'keith hammond'

Bookwire.com
'keith hammond'

Amazon:
'keith hammond' or 'book title'

Goodreads.com:
'keith hammond' or 'book title'

Reminder:
The best way to get an overall view of more than 80 books I've written, is to download the full-color, interactive catalog from our website.

LessonsForLifeBooks.com/catalog.html

Every book page has a link to the preview of that book, and includes ISBN info, ordering info, etc.

COMING SOON

ROMANCE 102
Are You Really Ms. Right?

REMEMBER:

> your *Choices*,
>
> the *Characteristics* you look for,
>
> any *Compromises* you are willing to make,
>
> helping to *Conform* his past behavior,
>
> and learning about your areas of *Compatibility*,

all lead up to a simple *Challenge* to teach your Mr. Right, using the concept of learned behavior and proven strategies, how to be and stay romantic, and enable you to measure his progress using the *Charts* I've outlined in this book.

Happy Reading!

Keith Hammond

To the women who want to know their men.

To the men who need to know their women.